THE MODERN HOMESTEAD GARDEN

Brimming with creative inspiration, how-to projects, and useful information to enrich your everyday life, Quarto Knows is a favorite destination for those pursuing their interests and passions. Visit our site and dig deeper with our books into your area of interest: Quarto Creates, Quarto Cooks, Quarto Homes, Quarto Lives, Quarto Drives, Quarto Explores, Quarto Gifts, or Quarto Kids.

© 2021 Quarto Publishing Group USA Inc.
Text © 2021 Gary Pilarchik

First Published in 2021 by Cool Springs Press, an imprint of The Quarto Group, 100 Cummings Center, Suite 265-D, Beverly, MA 01915, USA.
T (978) 282-9590 F (978) 283-2742 QuartoKnows.com

Cool Springs Press titles are also available at discount for retail, wholesale, promotional, and bulk purchase. For details, contact the Special Sales Manager by email at specialsales@quarto.com or by mail at The Quarto Group, Attn: Special Sales Manager, 100 Cummings Center, Suite 265-D, Beverly, MA 01915, USA.

25 24 23 22 21   2 3 4 5

ISBN: 978-0-7603-6817-6

Digital edition published in 2021
eISBN: 978-0-7603-6818-3

Library of Congress Cataloging-in-Publication Data

Pilarchik, Gary, author.
The modern homestead garden : growing self-sufficiency in any size backyard / Gary Pilarchik.
Beverly, MA : Cool Springs Press, 2021. |
Includes index.
ISBN 9780760368176 (trade paperback) | ISBN 9780760368183 (ebook)
1. Vegetable gardening. 2. Container gardening.
LCC SB324.4 .P55 2021 (print) | LCC SB324.4 (ebook) | DDC 635--dc23

LCCN 2020038465 (print) | LCCN 2020038466 (ebook)

Design: Amy Sly
Cover Image: Shutterstock
Page Layout: Amy Sly

Printed in China

Photography by Gary Pilarchik: Pages 4, 6, 12, 13, 15, 16, 21-23, 24 (top), 25, 28-30, 32-40, 42-44, 46 (right), 47 (top), 48 (left), 50, 56, 57 (top), 58-61, 63, 67, 85-96, 99, 104, 106 (right), 117, 118, 122, 125 (bottom), 127, 128, 130-134, 138-143, 158

Images via Shutterstock: Pages 7-11, 14, 17-20, 24 (bottom), 26, 27, 31, 41, 45, 46 (left), 47 (bottom row), 48 (right), 49, 51, 52, 54, 57 (bottom), 62, 70, 71, 77-84, 98, 100-103, 105, 106 (left), 107-116, 120, 123, 124, 125 (top row), 126, 129, 136, 144-152

THE MODERN HOMESTEAD GARDEN

GARY PILARCHIK

GROWING SELF-SUFFICIENCY IN ANY SIZE BACKYARD

COOL
SPRINGS
PRESS

PREFACE
MY GRAND-POP TAUGHT ME EARLY

I was first taught how to grow tomatoes and cucumbers as a grade-school child. My grandfather had a beautiful garden, and he would come to our house the week after Mother's Day to turn the soil and plant tomatoes. He had a special process for planting them, and each year he taught me his technique. I didn't realize I was learning. All I remember is having a great time putting stuff into the ground. It wasn't until I became older that I realized the principles of gardening he had taught me. He would always say, *We're just helping Nature along*. After the tomatoes and cucumbers were planted, my mom and I would add to the garden. Before I knew it, our garden was fully planted. Massive weeds would eventually come, but the garden still produced!

As a kid, I can't say I tended the garden or really appreciated it for what it was or for its worth. In fact, being told to weed was nothing less than torture. What I did learn was that vegetables came from plants that grew out of the ground. Planting a vegetable garden, to me, was fun and easy. My grandfather taught me all I needed to know. He gave me a lifelong hobby and ignited a passion.

I always loved planting with Grand-Pop. It's the primary memory I hold of him, and it's something that became a part of me. I still can see him in his light blue spring jacket, the left pocket always filled with dog biscuits—and our dog knew it! She would run right to his left hand and stare until she got a treat. Every year he'd carry the same blue coffee can of what he called "sweetener" (I know now it was garden lime). He would also be holding a brown paper grocery bag filled with transplant packs

of beefsteak tomatoes. You could smell the tomatoes as soon as the plants were pulled out of the bag. It's a smell I never tire of and it signals the start of each new gardening season. Soon, you and your family will have memories of growing together like mine.

In this book you'll find the principles and information you need to begin building a homestead garden of your own and start your journey toward becoming more self-sufficient. There are a thousand ways to plant a garden, and they all require you to tend the earth and get your hands dirty. Now, more than ever, it's important to learn how to grow food and develop the skills to become self-reliant. It's equally important to teach our children and grandchildren where food comes from and how to grow it.

—Gary Pilarchik

INTRODUCTION
WHAT IS A MODERN HOMESTEAD GARDEN?

Modern homesteading is about actively engaging in a more self-sufficient life-style within the everyday demands of modern life. You don't need to leave your community or move off-grid to have a homestead. People homestead in city apartments, urban backyards, community open spaces, and suburban homes, as well as on rural acreage. The idea of making changes to become more self-reliant can be overwhelming because homesteading can cover so many different areas of our lives, from the foods we eat and the clothes we wear to the energy we use and the resources we utilize. It's tough to know where to start. But the most important step is the first one. Start small, do what you can, and move at your own pace.

If you aren't sure where to start, the easiest first step in your journey toward greater self-sufficiency is to learn how to grow some of your own food. Take what-ever space your yard offers you, no matter how big or small, and slowly begin creating a landscape of herbs, fruits, and vegetables. You can grow food on decks, patios, porches, and balconies, not just in large in-ground garden plots. There are no size or location requirements for a homestead. As long as your goal is to increase your food self-sufficiency, you're homestead gardening. You'll find some of my favorite plants to grow and information to help set up your modern homestead garden and successfully care for it.

Growing, cooking, and sharing the food you grow is what a more self-suffi-cient life is all about. Modern homestead gardening is a new mindset and an approach to life that will not only help you transform your land into gardens but will also make you less reliant on the industrial food chain. The grocery store will become your *second* stop after you've walked your land and harvested your own homegrown seasonal crops.

Enjoy the ever-changing journey as you transform your home and its sur-roundings into an edible landscape. Let's open the door together, step outside, and begin.

1

BUILDING
YOUR FIRST
GARDEN

NATURE DESIGNED PLANTS TO THRIVE and bear fruits for future generations. All we have to do is give them most of what they need, most of the time. We don't need to be perfect or exact; we just have to design gardens thoughtfully to best meet the needs of the plants growing there. A plant needs sunlight, good soil, water, and nutrients, which Nature pretty much provides to a significant degree. As gardeners, we want to maximize our land and resources to consistently provide these things. We can start by maximizing sunlight.

Sunlight

Place garden beds where they receive the most direct sunlight. Generally speaking, the areas you select for your gardens should get a minimum of six hours of *direct sunlight* each day; the optimal amount is eight to ten hours. Direct sun means the sun's rays directly contact your garden plants. If your land is flat and open with no trees or structures, you can pretty much place your garden where you wish. You'll naturally have full southern exposure. Depending on the time of year, southern exposure gardens will get eight to twelve hours of direct sun. Unfortunately, many of us don't have a flat, open space that always gets full sun.

If you have trees, structures, or other obstacles, understanding how the sun tracks across the sky will help you place your garden. First, use a compass (or a smartphone, which often has a compass) to figure out where north, east, south, and west are. Keep in mind where shade falls from trees and other structures as the sun moves across your land. If you are designing a garden in fall or winter, imagine the trees with leaves on them and how they'll cast shade. The easiest way to figure out where to place your garden is to face south (east will be to your left and west will be to your right). The sun will move from your left as morning sun, in front of you as midafternoon sun, and to your right as afternoon sun. If you have the potential of shade falling onto your garden at times, total how many hours of direct sun falls onto the areas that you're considering as potential garden beds.

The best way to pick the right spot is to go out the potential garden areas at 8 a.m., 10 a.m., 12 p.m., 2 p.m., and 4 p.m. You want direct sun present in three of those two-hour time periods, totaling the minimum of 6 hours. The best sun, generally, is from 10 a.m. to 2 p.m. That's when the sun is at its highest point and strongest intensity, and it benefits plants the most. When possible, I recommend placing your gardens where those four hours of optimal sun will reach them.

Soil

Soil will vary greatly depending on where you live. There's no immediate need to strive to have perfect garden soil to start; don't let that concern become a barrier to starting. If grass, weeds, trees, bushes, and other plants are growing around the area where you want to start your gardens, then the earth's good enough. Something is already growing there, after all.

Building and maintaining garden soil begins when you start growing your first crops and continues every year thereafter. It never ends. We could talk at length about clay, sandy, and rocky soils and what makes perfect soil, but the bottom line is, you're going to build up the earth in your garden over time. No gardener starts with perfect, nutrition-dense soil. Instead, they build it slowly over time by regularly giving it what it needs. The most important thing to understand about a potential garden site is good drainage. While we can build up the quality of soil year after year, it is often

Start Small and Grow Your Confidence First

You don't need to build your entire garden at once. You don't even need a plan. All you need is a general vision. Buy some potting mix and a few containers or flower boxes, and if you are digging in the ground, build a single 4- by 4-foot (120 by 120 cm) bed. Plant a few seeds of things that interest you. Your motivation and excitement will grow as your homestead space begins to transform into a garden. Turning and touching the earth is how the journey begins. There's no other way to do it.

difficult—but not impossible—to manage poorly draining soils. One of the best ways to address problems is before they begin. Most garden plant root systems don't like sitting in overly soggy soil for prolonged periods as that can lead to problems. Plant roots and much beneficial soil microbiology need oxygen to thrive. Soil that has standing water interferes with the exchange of oxygen.

If your garden doesn't drain well after a heavy rain, water fills the air spaces in the soil and, over time, the roots die due to lack of oxygen. This is commonly known as "root rot." If you have a sloping landscape, place the garden higher on the slope and not toward the bottom. You don't want garden soil that's always soggy.

If you're not sure about how well your soil drains, dig a 12- by 12-inch (30 by 30 cm) hole and fill it with water from a hose. If it drains within an hour, you're on the right track. Fill it a second time; if it drains within an hour again, your site selection will be fine. Poorly drained soils are a bigger issue in some regions than others, but it's what I consider one of the most important factors in garden spot selection. Watching where water runs along your property after a strong thunderstorm can also help identify a garden site. If all you have is poorly draining soil, it's best to know that from the beginning so you can act accordingly. If that's an issue, raised beds are the answer (more on setting up a raised bed garden in chapter 5).

The Value of Compost

Composting, addressed in chapter 4, is the answer to building and maintaining outstanding garden soil year after year. Creating compost is a great way to use resources on your homestead. Using resources on-hand as a way to save money and improve the production of your garden is part of self-sufficiency in a modern homestead garden. Composting takes work and the costs are effort and time, but the payoffs are large and important. Bagged composts and similar materials are not only expensive, but they're often poor quality. Compost has macronutrients and micronutrients, and it provides organic matter. It has everything Nature intended to feed plants and soil life. After reading this book, you'll be able to build up, replenish, and improve your garden soil each season by using homemade compost.

Plants and Soil pH Levels

Another factor to consider when it comes to healthy soil is its pH value. Yes, the level of your soil's pH is important, but it's not something to overly worry about when you're just getting started. Compost is Nature's pH regulator and regular use will address any pH concerns over time. Most garden vegetables do extremely well in a pH range of 5.5 to 7.0. Vegetables adapt—they want to grow—and compost helps balance overly acidic or alkaline soils. Generally speaking, compost is pH neutral and all garden plants love it. If you get to a point where certain vegetables aren't thriving or doing well, perform a soil test to determine its pH level. If your soil is too acidic, you can add lime to raise the pH level to a better range. If your soil is too alkaline, you can add peat moss or other acidifiers to bring the alkalinity level or pH level down. Again, this is something to address if it becomes a problem. The best way to deal with a problem is to prevent it, and regularly using compost is the solution. Remember, if the area you selected for you gardens has grass, weeds, and other plants already growing in it, the soil is good enough to start your garden. I have never done a pH test throughout all of my gardening years. Compost works that well!

VEGETABLE PH PREFERENCES

Vegetable	pH Range for Growing
Asparagus	6.0–8.0
Bean	6.0–7.5
Beet	6.0–7.5
Broccoli	6.0–7.0
Brussels Sprouts	6.0–7.5
Cabbage	6.0–7.0
Carrot	6.0–7.0
Cauliflower	5.5–7.5
Celery	5.5–7.0
Cucumber	5.5–7.0
Garlic	5.5–8.0
Kale	6.0–7.5
Lettuce	6.0–7.0
Peas	6.0–7.5
Pepper	5.5–7.0
Potato	5.0–6.5
Pumpkin	5.5–7.5
Radish	6.0–7.0
Spinach	6.0–7.5
Squash	6.0–7.5
Tomato	5.5–7.5
Turnip	5.5–7.0

Sweet and Sour: The pH Scale

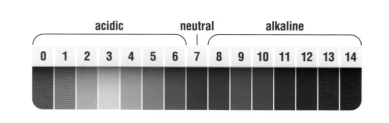

As I mentioned in the preface, my grandfather carried a coffee can full of lime around the garden. He called it "sweetener" and said it would fix "sour" soil. "Sour," in the garden world, refers to soil that's acidic and "sweet" refers to soil that's alkaline. Think of vinegar (sour) and baking soda (sweet). When you mix them, they react with each other and fizz like crazy. Eventually they neutralize each other and what's left is liquid with a more neutral pH level. As my grand-pop said, you can use sweetener on sour soil, which is what he did when adding lime to his garden. To clarify, he never carried a container of "sour" because the soil where he lived was already naturally acidic, but the principle would be the same. "Sweet" soil can be "soured" (made more acidic) by using something such as elemental sulfur or aluminum sulfate to lower the soil's pH into the acidic range. Regardless, the goal is to maintain a more neutral level of pH between 5.5 to 7 in our garden beds.

Temperature

Temperature affects the way plants grow and dictates when and what you plant. While we can't control daily or seasonal temperatures in our homestead gardens (only Nature can do that), we *can* control how we use our growing conditions to maximize our harvest. Some plants prefer cool weather and cool soil. Other plants prefer warmer temperatures and warm soil.

Associated with daily temperature is the length of your area's growing season. The primary growing season for outdoor production is typically from the last frost date in spring to the first frost date in fall. It's possible to extend your season using cold frames or row covers. For example, my growing season runs from early April through early November. These two dates give you a general idea of the length of your growing season, which is how you'll base planting your homestead garden.

If you're just starting out, you don't need an extensive planting plan in hand. You can plant, as most of us do, in this order: cool-weather crops, followed by warm-weather crops, and then, if your season is long enough and depending on the vegetables you choose to grow, more cool-weather crops. If you live in a hot climate that doesn't get freezing temperatures, you may not be able to grow some cool-season vegetables, but you have greater access to growing more warm-weather vegetables and fruits.

When planning and planting your garden, you have to grow what will mature within a given temperature timeframe. We have cool temperature spans and warm temperature spans. For example, some varieties of cool-season crops, such as lettuce and radishes, need twenty-eight to forty days of cooler temperatures to mature. When you plant seeds or transplants, you want to know you will have at least that many days of the appropriate temperature range. Other cool-season vegetables such as broccoli need sixty-five to ninety days to mature. If soil warms as the heads of broccoli are forming, you won't be able to harvest a mature crown. Instead, the plant moves into flower production. Cool temperatures let the flower buds mature slowly to a nice harvesting size without the buds opening. We plant based on the temperatures our crops prefer and how long it takes for them to mature. We have to match the needed maturation period of a plant to a timeframe of supporting temperatures.

Warm-weather plants, such as tomatoes, peppers, and summer squash, die or are damaged when night temperatures drop below freezing. Many cool-weather crops, such as lettuces, change their growth habits based on temperature. Instead of producing

sweet leafy greens, as they do during cool temperatures, the leaves become bitter and the plants bolt (go to flower) when the warm weather arrives. Their growth habit changes with the temperature changes. Other plant varieties shut down and slow growth when temperatures reach prolonged periods of 95°F (35°C) and warmer. Tomatoes, for instance, will drop their blossoms and sometimes drop small fruit when temperature remain in the upper 90s (30s) and higher for prolonged periods. This is likely a survival instinct for the plant. Producing fruit takes a lot of energy and resources, so when plants are heat-stressed, they usually stop producing until ideal temperatures and conditions return.

Generally speaking, you can look at the temperature zone (average monthly temperatures) of your growing area and calculate when to plant cool-weather crops and warm-weather crops, and if you can plant cool-weather crops again toward the end of the season. The timing and length of each season varies across all of our gardens. Cool-weather crops typically enjoy 40°F to 50°F (5°C to 10°C) nights and 60°F to 70°F (16°C to 21°C) days. Warm-weather crops like 60°F to 70°F (16°C to 21°C) nights and 70°F to 80°F (21°C to 27°C) days. We plant gardens based on soil and ambient temperatures. The next chapter highlights different vegetables in each category in greater detail and tells you how to make them part of your homestead garden, from planting to harvest.

Length of Growing Season

The length of your growing season is generally affected by freezing temperatures, but prolonged periods of heat can also affect crops. While some crops can take a light frost and freeze, they don't grow well if temperatures regularly fall below 32°F (0°C). Warm-weather crops will be damaged or killed by a frost. Again, a growing season is typically your area's last average frost date all the way to your first frost date. Some gardens

may only have two or three months to really grow and produce. Other gardens may have six or seven months of production. Rarely does a garden have the entire year to produce. The bottom line is, planting and harvesting will vary based on your geographical area. Understanding the length of your growing season helps in planning when to start seeds indoors and/or in a greenhouse and when to get them out into the garden (chapter 3). It may dictate the need for cold frames or hoop houses to extend your growing season. It may also help you decide whether it's best to grow in containers (chapter 5), earth beds, or raised beds (chapter 6). Each type of garden has benefits and you can choose one or all of them. I use them all and have a long growing season as a result.

Garden Journaling

I keep a journal with me. I write notes a couple times a week, such as planting dates, seed varieties, and even notes on the soil amendments I'm using. These are just short notes to help me remember come late fall and winter when I'm looking for something to do. I might mark down fertilizers or jot down new things I try. While a journal is great for so many things, the key is to mark down the planting dates for different warm- and cool-season crops. This will help you figure out when the best time to transplant into the garden or to sow seeds is. I've been trying to grow fall Brussels sprouts, broccoli, and cauliflower. My first recorded attempt was putting transplants out in late August, but that wasn't enough time for them to fully mature. By tracking the dates, I now know to plant them in late July this year.

Types of Gardens: Containers, Raised Beds, and Earth Beds

Now that you know more about setting your homestead garden up for success by understanding some of the basic principles of site selection, soil, temperature, and sunlight, it's time to look at different ways to grow. Not all homestead gardens have to be in the ground. You can start small and expand over time. The growing options that are best for you depend on your space, the amount of time you have to tend your garden, your budget, and other factors. Essentially you have three choices: containers, raised beds, and earth beds. We'll take a look at each so you can make a choice and get started. Later chapters provide detailed information about growing using each of these methods.

GROWING IN CONTAINERS

Container gardening is a great way to start learning about growing and tending your own plants. Containers are perfect for herb gardens, and many vegetables and fruits also do well in containers, especially compact or dwarf varieties. I keep a container garden near my kitchen and also use them out in my main garden. The primary concerns when growing in containers are making sure you have the right soil and keeping plants watered. If a container dries out completely—even once—it greatly damages the plant's root systems and that affects its overall growth and production. Chapter 6 is dedicated entirely to growing in containers. You'll find lots of information to make container gardening successful.

GROWING IN RAISED BEDS

Raised beds frame the area in which you are going to plant. I recommend keeping the width of raised beds at 4 feet (1.2 m). The reason is that your arms are about 2 feet (0.6 m) long; therefore, you can reach into the garden space to tend plants without walking on the growing area. No walking means you don't compact the soil under your weight, the soil stays aerated, and you don't have to turn and loosen the soil in the bed every season.

GROWING IN EARTH BEDS

Earth beds can be used in small or very large gardens. Earth beds are typically slightly mounded, but they can also be flat. You can build 10- to 100-foot (3- to 30.5-m) rows that vary in widths of 3, 4, or 5 feet (0.9, 1.2, or 1.5 m). Between the rows, sit your walking and tending paths. Mounding the soil helps drainage, planting, and cultivation. You don't need a large space to grow in earth beds; you can grow a lot of plants in a small garden footprint. Chapter 5 walks you through more of the ins and outs of setting up your homestead garden in earth beds and raised beds. It will be a more useful chapter to you if this is the growing method you choose.

Containers, raised beds, and earth beds are all effective ways to grow plants and build your gardens. I do a combination of all three. You'll get more information about these techniques in coming chapters, but you don't have to settle on just one. The goal of this overview is to help you realize you can start your garden homestead many ways. Building a garden is like sculpting in the earth. You start with a blank slate. I simply love it and modify my garden spaces every year.

Start Small and Learn

Don't get overwhelmed and feel you have to start with a large garden. It is more important just to start and select a garden size you can fully manage and enjoy. The homestead mindset is moving in a direction to become more self-sufficient, and that really starts by actively growing and learning. Your journey can begin with single small garden bed or a couple of flower boxes.

Expand your gardens and homestead as you learn, gain confidence, and find more space. Becoming more self-sufficient doesn't mean you must do *everything* from the start.

Now that you've had a general introduction to modern homestead gardening, let's dig into the details of planning and planting your space.

Outside the Garden Box

Perhaps you live in an apartment or a townhouse or your current home is nothing but trees and shade. Ask yourself this question, *Where else can I have a garden?* Ask family and friends who have land to work with you. You might build and tend the garden, they'll provide the land, and you'll share the harvest. Be creative as you move toward your vision of the perfect homestead. Ask churches or shelters for land and offer fresh produce for people in need. Many areas have community gardens where you can rent space. If you're in a city there are often neglected spaces. Partner with a local nonprofit organization to clean up a neglected space and build gardens.

Places to Grow a Garden

- Balcony
- Back porch
- Backyard or front yard
- Neighbors' yards

- Family members' yards
- Community garden
- Church or nonprofit organization
- Restaurants

- Local community businesses
- Schools

2

PLANTING
YOUR GARDEN
AND THE BEST
VEGETABLES
TO GROW

THERE ARE SO MANY DIFFERENT HERBS, FRUITS, vegetables, and flowers to grow on your homestead. It's easy to become overwhelmed when deciding what, when, and how to grow them. You'll hear terms such as frost dates; crop types; heirloom, hybrid, and organic seeds; and genetically modified organisms, or GMOs—some of which you just learned about but others that may be a mystery. I'll help you decipher and understand these terms as you learn to navigate the world of garden transplants and seeds. As discussed in the previous chapter, plants vary on when they go into the ground based on temperatures.

In this chapter, I'll highlight some mainstay vegetable plants for the homestead garden and discuss basic planting principles for each. I could write extensively on how to plant, but the bottom line is that experience is the best teacher. Remember, the same bean seed will grow whether it's planted ¼ or ½ inch (0.6 or 1 cm) deep. Some of the best bean plants I've grown were seeds that fell from the previous season's pods. The seeds just sat on the ground through months of freezing temperatures. When the conditions were right,

they sprouted, took hold, and grew where they fell. I was not involved. They just followed the path of Nature. This is something I want you to remember: seeds want to sprout and plants want to grow. Everything you read about sowing seeds and planting transplants are variations of just one thing: putting them in soil. Exact timing, depth, spacing, watering, and so on varies from book to book and internet search to search. But as Grand-Pop told me, "Just get them in the ground."

The Modern Homestead Garden Attitude

The first thing that happens when people think about having a homestead garden is doubt. They may think it's too difficult to manage a vegetable garden or they let others convince them they don't have enough skill or land. The bottom line is: Don't doubt yourself, *challenge* yourself. And don't let other people tell you what you can or can't do. It's better to try, learn, and see

what happens. That is so much better than looking back and regretting that you never even tried.

The modern homestead garden is not about the amount of land you have; it's more about changing your perspective on the way to live. It is about how we see our lives, our families, our homes, and how we use our land. Our homes are more than places to be in-between work. They're places to raise a family, build memories, and become more self-sufficient in the ways we live our lives. It is a never-ending process that we get better at each year.

Popular Warm-Weather Crops

- Corn
- Basil
- Bean
- Cantaloupe
- Cucumber
- Eggplant
- Okra

- Peppers
- Pumpkin
- Summer Squash
- Sweet Potato
- Tomato
- Watermelon

I've grouped the featured plants based on their preferred growing season. As you know, some are planted in fall or early spring when the ground and air are cool. These cool-season plants shrug off a frost without being damaged. Warm-season crops go into the ground during the warmth of early summer. I selected some of my favorite vegetable plants from both categories to get you started. I'll walk you through the skills necessary for planting them in your garden. One goal as you build and grow your homestead garden is to have a continuous harvest through spring, summer, fall, and even into winter. The only way to figure out what works best in your area is to get planting, keep notes, and add new vegetables and fruits each year. I still make mistakes and learn; just enjoy the process and the rewards.

Growing and Planting Warm-Weather Crops

Warm-weather crops prefer 50°F to 55°F (10°C to 13°C) soil and thrive when temperatures are 60°F to 70°F (16 °C to 21°C) at night and 70°F to 80°F (21°C to 27°C) during the day. Putting warm-weather crop transplants into the ground when the days are getting warmer but the soil temperature is still below 50°F (10°C) will only get you

plants that sit there and struggle. They don't like cold soil and cannot tolerate frost. Even a light frost will damage their leaves. If you plant seeds, they will sit dormant as they wait for the right temperature conditions to germinate. Be patient and wait for warm rains and a couple weeks of the right temperatures to warm the soil before you put warm-weather plants into your garden.

There is no absolute set way to grow vegetables; each crop is different. There is no need to worry about exact planting distance or seed depth. I'll provide a few basic ways to plant each of the different vegetables featured here, and you can develop your own planting style. For example, I've grown tomato plants 1 foot (30 cm) apart, 2 feet (60 cm) apart, and 3 feet (90 cm) apart. I've grown them in containers, closely planted together as hedges, and in well-spaced-out rows. I have even let them sprawl wildly across the ground. In all cases I've always gotten plenty of tomatoes. Use my advice as basic guidance, but never feel you have to use it as a rule.

DAYS TO MATURITY OF POPULAR WARM-WEATHER CROPS

Crop	Days to Maturity
Bean	65–75
Corn	65–90
Cucumber	50–65
Eggplant	75–90
Melon (Musk/Cantaloupe)	80–90
Okra	55–65
Peppers	65–100
Pumpkin	85–120
Squash	40–55
Tomatillo	65–100
Tomato (Determinate)	55–80
Tomato (Indeterminate)	75–100
Watermelon	80–90
Zucchini	40–55

Determining the Maturity Date

The maturity date (also called days to maturity) can be confusing when getting started. It's defined as the amount of time a plant needs to mature before it can be harvested. The maturity date of a particular variety is noted in its seed catalog description, on the seed packet, or on the pot tag at the nursery. The maturity date often comes as a range of days, say sixty-five to seventy-five days as an example. When planting seeds directly into the garden, the maturity date is based on when the seeds germinate. But for plants that commonly go into the ground as transplants, the maturity date is based on when the plants are put into the ground. aTransplants tend to reach maturity before direct-sown seeds, and that's why we often start seeds indoors. A seed can sit in the soil a long time before germinating. Don't start counting days to maturity until the seed breaks the soil surface.

tomatoes

Tomatoes are warm-weather crops and are probably grown in some form or fashion in most gardens. They are always ranked as the number one garden vegetable. I'll discuss how you can start tomatoes indoors and grow your own transplants. Transplants give you a jump on the season; using 6- to 8-week-old transplants is a great way to plant tomatoes where you have a shorter summer or warm period. You'll learn more about growing from seed indoors, planting seeds directly outdoors, and using transplants in chapter 3.

The general rule for spacing tomatoes as seeds or transplants is 2 to 3 feet (60 to 90 cm) apart. If you're planting tomatoes for the first time, I recommend planting them 3 feet (90 cm) apart as it will be easier to manage the plants.

Growing Tomatoes

Crop Type: Warm-Season

Average Soil Planting Temperature:
Seeds: 65°F (18°C)
Transplants: 50°F (10°C)

Transplants: Start 6 to 8 weeks before the ideal outdoor soil temperature arrives.

Direct Seeding: Plant 2 seeds per hole ¼ to ½ inch (0.6 to 1 cm) deep. Cover and water them in well. Thin seedlings to 1 plant when they are 3 inches (7.5 cm) tall.

Plant Spacing: 2 to 3 feet (60 to 90 cm) apart

Growing Tips: Keep additional nitrogen to a minimum after plants are established. A lower-nitrogen water-soluble fertilizer is recommended for tomatoes when you see the first fruit setting. Continued high levels of nitrogen can lead to excess leaf growth, which can lead to insect and disease problems. Water-soluble feeding after a heavy harvest is beneficial.

Tomato plants can be planted 1 to 2 feet (60 to 90 cm) apart and even grown as hedges. More vigilance is needed to manage potential pests and diseases, but the benefit is larger harvest in less space.

Container Tips: Grow determinate variety tomatoes in 5-gallon (19 L) containers. For indeterminate tomatoes, 10-gallon (38 L) containers work best. Only 1 plant per container.

I have grown up to sixty different varieties of tomatoes in my garden over a single season. There is nothing I enjoy more than starting tomatoes from seed indoors and finding new varieties to grow. Seed-starting indoors opens your growing experience to thousands of different plant varieties that you will never find in stores. I keep notes in my journal about what plants thrive and what plants dive. Varieties I recommend are the 'Homestead', 'Jubilee', 'Marglobe', 'Cherokee Purple', 'Small Cherry', and 'Black Cherry', which are all great for beginners. They have good disease-resistance, produce well, and bring color to your garden.

Determinate and Indeterminate Tomato Characteristics

Tomato varieties usually fall into two types. The first is "determinate" and the other is "indeterminate." Determinate tomatoes usually produce first, fifty-five to eighty days from transplanting. A determinate plant grows to a height predetermined by the plant's genetics and sets most of its flowers over a short period. That means you get a lot of early tomatoes over a two- to three-week period. After the plant produces, growth slows to the point of almost dying back. I often remove my determinate tomato varieties at this point and plant new determinate tomato transplants—not seeds—in their place. You can plant a second wave if you have a good seventy-five days or more of the right temperatures.

Indeterminate tomatoes continue to grow, flower, and set fruit throughout an entire growing season and only stop when disease or cold stops them. They generally need seventy-five to one hundred days to start producing. If you have a lot of larger green tomatoes as frost approaches, pick them green and make fried green tomatoes.

I recommend growing determinate tomato varieties in containers and as the first tomatoes to put in your garden beds. A great way to have a continuous harvest is to mix determinate and indeterminate varieties throughout your homestead garden. I also recommend mixing tomato varieties that produce cherry-type tomatoes, medium-, and large-sized tomatoes. The larger tomatoes that can weigh 12 ounces (115 g) to well over 1 pound (455 g) can take ninety days or more to ripen. While you wait, other tomatoes are ready for harvest.

A First Tomato Garden

One standard red cherry indeterminate
One colored cherry indeterminate
One 4- to 6-ounce (115 to 170 g) red determinate
One 4- to 6-ounce (115 to 170 g) colored determinate
One 6- to 8-ounce (170 to 225 g) red indeterminate
One 8- to 12-ounce (225 to 340 g) colored indeterminate
One 16-ounce-plus (455 g plus) indeterminate

There are so many different tomato varieties. The best way to introduce yourself to the world of growing your own tomatoes is to mix up varieties. You'll get early tomatoes from the determinate tomatoes. Cherry tomatoes will brilliantly cover the entire plant, and you'll have enough tomatoes over the season to share with family and friends. I also recommended a single plant that produces 1 pound (455 g) and larger tomatoes. You'll enjoy watching them grow and maybe even enjoy showing off a bit to whomever comes to your homestead.

peppers

I grow dozens of different pepper varieties in my garden, some hot and some sweet. They are one of my favorite vegetables to eat and to start indoors. Pepper plants actually become woody shrubs if you live in a frost-free area. If you live in a frost zone, you can dig up pepper plants, put them in containers, and overwinter them in a greenhouse. As warm weather returns, plant them back in the ground, and you'll get larger plants, early fruiting, and more production. However, most of us don't have a greenhouse that holds temperatures above freezing.

Peppers take time to mature. Some varieties will produce seventy-five days from transplant, but many take ninety days and longer. In most of our gardens, pepper plants will die out at the end of the season. For that reason, and the fact that pepper plants can take a good ninety days to fully mature and produce, pepper seeds should be started indoors. I recommend starting seeds eight to twelve weeks before the outdoor soil is regularly 50°F (10°C) and the danger of frost has passed in your area.

Growing Peppers

Crop Type: Warm-Season

Average Soil Planting Temperature:
Seeds: 65°F (18°C)
Transplants: 50°F (10°C)

Transplants: Start 8 to 10 weeks before your area's target outdoor soil temperature arrives.

Direct Seeding: Plant 2 seeds per hole ¼ to ½ inch (0.6 to 1 cm) deep. Cover and water them in well. Thin seedlings to 1 plant when plants have 4 sets of leaves.

Plant Spacing: 18 to 24 inches (45 to 60 cm) apart

Growing Tips: Like tomatoes, keep additional nitrogen to a minimum after plants are established. A lower-nitrogen water-soluble fertilizer is recommended for peppers. Continued use of high levels of nitrogen can lead to wonderful leaf growth but pepper production can suffer.

You can also place 2 peppers in a single planting hole when spacing plants 18 inches (45 cm) or more apart.

Container Tips: Use 1 plant per 5 gallons (19 L) of space as a guideline.

Scoville Units Measure Peppers' Heat

You can grow sweet peppers in different colors, shapes, and sizes. You can also grow hot peppers with different flavors and heat levels, which is measured in Scoville units. While we may be accustomed to the 'Jalapeño' and cayenne pepper Scoville ratings of about 3,000 Scoville units, very few of us have tried ghost peppers or scorpion peppers, which have a Scoville rating of over 1,000,000, and for good reason—they are too hot!

'Carolina Reaper': 1,500,000

'Ghost Pepper' (Bhut Jolokia Red): 1,000,000

'Caribbean Red': 400,000–450,000

'Jamaican Yellow': 300,000

'Scotch Bonnet Orange': 200,000–300,000

Habanero Types: 150,000–325,000

'Thai Hot': 80,000

'Red Cayenne': 30,000–50,000

'Tabasco': 30,000–50,000

'Hot Lemon': 5,000–30,000

'Hot Portugal': 5,000

'Hot Cherry': 3,500–6,000

'Jalapeño': 3,500–6,000

Poblano: 500–2,500

'Red Chili': 500–750

Sweet Peppers: 0–50

My Favorite Pepper Varieties

I like growing moderately hot peppers as they have a lot of flavor and tolerable heat. One of my favorite peppers is the 'Poblano', which I highly recommend. I also like the 'Facing Heaven' pepper or Szechuan varieties for drying and making hot pepper flakes. The standard sweet pepper found in most gardens is the banana pepper because it's an early and prolific producer. As much as I enjoy growing heirloom peppers and vegetables, I also enjoy growing some of the sweeter variety hybrid peppers. Some hybrids have almost a candylike sweetness. I had a chance to learn about the care and time it takes breeders to create and successfully cross two pepper plants. It's a labor of love; breeders have my respect.

squash and zucchini

Squash and zucchini are must-have warm-weather vegetables. Squash are technically fruits, but we grow and know them as vegetables. There are so many different varieties to grow. They fall into the categories either of summer squash or winter squash. We commonly use the terms "squash" and "zucchini" interchangeably, but zucchini is technically a type of summer squash. The main difference is that summer squash don't store well, but they mature and produce more quickly than winter squash varieties. Winter squash, such as 'Acorn', 'Butternut', 'Spaghetti', or 'Blue Hubbard' varieties, store extremely well, and take longer to mature. Both types are grown during warm weather, but they're harvested at different times. Some winter squash can be stored for months. As you strive to become more self-sufficient, you'll want to have a mix of summer and winter squash. Reducing our dependence on purchased produce is partly why we have homestead gardens.

Squash come in different shades of green, yellow, white, blue, orange, and more. They can be striped and have multiple colors too. Squash vary in shapes and sizes from round to straight, crooked, bell, ribbed, and many more. Some may be picked at 8 ounces (225 g) while others are picked at several pounds or more. Some plants are more bush-like, as with summer squash, or vine-like, as with winter squash. These plants take up a lot of space in the garden, so it's important to give them what they need to grow well.

Squash plants can be affected by diseases such as powdery mildew and also from insects such as the squash vine borer, though some varieties seem to be more susceptible to these problems than others. The best way to deal with these pests and diseases is to practice early prevention and begin treatment before the diseases and pests arrive. Each garden will have different disease and pest issues. Take notes and learn as each problem enters your garden. Stick with the plants that seem to do the best and replace varieties that are problematic.

Squash and zucchini grow extremely quickly from seed. The two reasons to start indoors are: you have a short growing season, or you're waiting for space to open up in your garden. If you grow them as transplants, plant outdoors two to three weeks after germination. Letting squash and zucchini sit beyond that timeframe will cause problems. Very often they quickly move to flower production and stop growing in the starting pots. You want flowering to start in the garden beds. For direct sowing, plant two seeds per hole and thin to the strongest plant when the first main leaves are established. I recommend a good 3 feet (90 cm) between plants. The plants get quite large, and this spacing allows better care and maintenance.

Summer squash can start producing thirty-five to forty-five days from seed once germinated. This fast growth and production can be used in your favor to help manage the diseases and pest problems they get. One strategy I use is to plant on a rotation. When the first squash or zucchini appear on the plants, I start more squash and zucchini in small pots for future transplant. If I have the space, I will direct sow new squash seeds away from the mature plants. This way, as diseases and pests take the mature plants, I have new plants on the way. This strategy works because many garden diseases and pests show up when conditions are right for them. Often this is a narrow window, which begins to close as you put out new plants or seeds. Don't be afraid to remove sickly plants. Remove, replace, and move on to the next garden chore. You'll find lots of advice on managing pests and diseases in your homestead garden in chapter 8.

Growing Squash and Zucchini

Crop Type: Warm-Season

Average Soil Planting Temperature:
Seeds: 65°F (18°C)
Transplants: 50°F (10°C)

Transplants: Start 4 weeks before your area's ideal outdoor soil temperature arrives.

Direct Seeding: Plant 2 seeds per hole 1 inch (2.5 cm) deep. Cover and water them in well. Thin seedlings to 1 plant when plants have 1 main leaf.

Plant Spacing: 3 feet (90 cm) apart

Growing Tips: Compost is the best way to fertilize these heavy feeders. A supplemental water-soluble fertilizer every 2 weeks will keep them green.

Container Tips: Grow only 1 bush-type summer squash plant in a container that is 10 gallons (38 L) or more. Squash plants are heavy consumers of water and nutrients.

cucumbers

Cucumbers have to be grown with tomatoes and onions if for no other reason than I love making a tomato and cucumber salad several times a week during summer. This bowl of heaven is what connects me to my garden year after year. I grew it, I made it, and I get to enjoy it.

There's nothing more uniquely flavorful and scented than freshly picked cucumbers. The fragrance and sweetness cannot be obtained through a cucumber purchased at a grocery store. Cucumbers do extremely well when sown directly into the garden. They grow quickly when the warmth of summer arrives. Like squash, you can start them indoors, but it is important to get transplants quickly into the ground. Growing two plants in one space helps with pollination and increases your homestead harvests.

Although you can let cucumber sprawl on the ground, I find they grow best if trained up a trellis. You can buy pickling variety cucumbers or grow the larger 8-inch (20 cm) cucumbers; I recommend both. Although cucumbers come in different shapes and sizes, sometimes even different colors and skin textures, they vary only slightly in flavor. They all have that uniquely delicious cucumber taste. I grow cucumbers in "waves." I put some out early in the season, and two weeks later after they've been growing, I start new transplants in pots. I get them in the ground about two weeks after germinating and continue putting new plants into the ground every four weeks. This method of succession planting provides a continuous supply of cucumbers as my older plants need to be removed for various reasons. I go through a lot of cucumbers. Did I mention tomato and cucumber salads?

Growing Cucumbers

Crop Type: Warm-Season

Average Soil Planting Temperature:
Seeds: 65°F (18°C)
Transplants: 50°F (10°C)

Transplants: Start 4 weeks before your area's ideal outdoor soil temperature arrives.

Direct Seeding: Plant 3 seeds per hole 1 inch (2.5 cm) deep. Cover and water them in well. Thin seedlings to 2 plants when the plants have 1 main leaf.

Plant Spacing: 2 to 3 feet (60 to 90 cm) apart

Growing Tips: Compost is the best way to fertilize these heavy feeders. A supplemental water-soluble fertilizer every 2 weeks will keep them green and producing. You can plant them more closely if you grow them vertically.

Container Tips: Grow 2 bush-type cucumber plants in a 10-gallon (38 L) container. They are heavy consumers of water and nutrients. They should be fertilized every 10 to 14 days with water-soluble fertilizer.

beans

We can end the warm-season crops with the vegetable plants I love to trellis all over my garden: beans.

Beans are a must-have for any homestead garden. They are typically labeled as pole (climbing) beans or as bush-type beans. 'Kentucky Wonder' pole bean is a standard choice for many gardeners. Pole beans can climb 10 to 20 feet (3 to 6 m) using their twining growth habit to wrap around support structures. They are perfect to grow on fences and up tall trellises. If you wonder how you reach the top of 20-foot (6-m) vine—you don't. When the runners get to 6 to 7 feet (1.8 to 2 m) high, start guiding or training them back downward. I recommend growing pole or climbing bean varieties whenever possible, if only to maximize space.

Green beans are very prolific, and you can harvest them for several months over the season. You can eat them raw, lightly sauté them, or dry them for long-term storage. One thing that's important, especially when working on becoming more self-sufficient, is storing food for winter, something I discuss in chapter 10. There are plenty of beans varieties that can be grown for drying and storing. They make wonderful protein sources during the cold months. Beans can be left to dry on the vines and then harvested when the shell is completely dry; harvest only after at least two consecutive sunny days. You want the beans to be dry when shelled and stored.

Growing Beans

Crop Type: Warm-Season

Average Soil Planting Temperature:
Seeds: 65°F
Transplants: 50°F

Transplants: I recommend direct seeding.

Direct Seeding: Plant seeds 1 inch (2.5 cm) deep, cover, and water them in well.

Plant Spacing: Plant bush beans 2 inches (5 cm) apart with 12 inches (30 cm) between rows. Plant pole beans in groups of 3 every 12 inches (30 cm).

Growing Tips: Beans should be harvested regularly. The more you pick, the more the plants will produce.

Container Tips: Grow 5 to 8 bush or pole bean plants per 10-gallon (38 L) container. If growing pole beans in a pot, erect a trellis for them to climb.

Growing and Planting Cool-Weather Crops

Most cool-weather crops can take a light frost and the plants won't be damaged. Some varieties can even take a heavier freeze. Cool-weather crops enjoy 40- to 50-degree (5°C to 10°C) nights and 60- to 70-degree (16°C to 21°C) days. Many of these crops will grow into and through the warm season but the warmth changes them. Consistently warm weather heats the soil and triggers bolting. The flavors of the leaves of some crops turn bitter when this change in growth occurs. Bolting is the process where many cool-weather crops, such as lettuces and other greens, stop producing leaves and start producing flowers to make seed. Consistently warm ambient air and soil temperatures and longer days are signals to reproduce.

MATURITY DATES FOR COMMON COOL-SEASON CROPS

Arugula: 30–40 days

Beet: 50–65 days. Leaves can be harvested sooner.

Broccoli: 65–75 days. Keep leaves on the plant once the main head is harvested and you will get side blooms to eat.

Bunching Onion: 55–75 days

Carrot: 55–75 days

Cauliflower: 65-75 days

Chard: 55–65 days

Collards: 55–60 days. Take leaves early as you wish.

Endive: 55–60 days. Take leaves early as you wish.

Garlic: Plant in fall for a late spring/early summer harvest.

Kale: 45–60 days

Kohlrabi: 55–65 days

Leek: 85–110 days. Can be planted in summer for a fall harvest.

Lettuce: 45–60 days

Mustard Greens: 30–50 days

Peas: 55–75 days

Potato: Plant in early spring and harvest early summer when the tops die back.

Radish: 25–40 days

Spinach: 35–50 days. Take leaves as you wish.

Turnip: 45–60 days

A long, cool season of the right temperatures allows plants to grow and mature properly for harvesting. These night and day temperatures also keep the soil cool. You need a long cool season for edible flower heads, such as broccoli and cauliflower, to get to full size without bolting. Cool-season crops are typically two-season crops; they can be planted in spring when you're coming out of the freeze of winter and they can be planted later in summer as you're entering into the cool temperatures of fall. The days to maturity chart suggests how many days of cool temperatures are needed to harvest different cool-weather crops.

peas

Peas are often first the seeds you can sow outdoors because they can be planted as soon as the soil can be worked. They don't like to sit in soggy, cold winter soil; they will rot. Make sure your garden soil is draining and no longer frozen before direct sowing peas. The air temperatures may be right, but your soil may not be ready. A great way to get an early crop of peas is by starting them in containers.

Pea leaves and shoots can handle a frost, and they need a good sixty days of cool weather to produce their best. The flowers and pods actually don't do well with frost but that's fine for spring peas as they're growing into warmer weather. Flowering comes later when it has warmed, but you have to time it right when you're growing them from summer into fall and frost is on the horizon. There are basically three types of peas that you can grow.

1. Shelling peas get their name for the act of removing the pea shell at harvest, using only the mature peas. The shells are not easily digested.

2. Snow peas are flat edible pods with immature peas inside the pod. The pod is eaten whole and is often used in stir fry dishes.

3. Sugar snap peas are plump peas inside a crisp edible seedpod. The entire pod is edible and sweet. You can't appreciate the true taste of sugar snap peas unless they are eaten fresh off the vine.

Growing Peas

Crop Type: Cool-Season

Average Soil Planting Temperature: 40°F to 50°F (4°C to 10°C)

Transplants: Start 2 to 3 weeks before planting them outdoors.

Direct Seeding: Plant seeds 2 inches (5 cm) apart and ½ inch (1 cm) deep. Cover and water them in well.

Plant Spacing: 2 inches (5 cm) apart and 4 to 6 inches (10 to 15 cm) between rows.

Growing Tips: Peas should be harvested regularly as overly mature peas are tough and not as sweet.

Container Tips: Grow 5 to 8 pea plants per 5-gallon (19 L) container. Use a trellis for them to climb.

You can plant peas in so many different ways. Always provide taller varieties with something to climb as they have hollow stems and are fragile. I enjoy planting peas in a square and putting tree branches throughout the square for them to trellis themselves upon. Don't make the square more than 4 by 4 feet (1.2 by 1.2 m) as you want to be able to reach into center of the square at harvest.

cauliflower and broccoli

I struggle to get cauliflower and broccoli to produce fully formed large heads in my homestead garden. These plants need a consistently long cool period with the right day and night temperatures. I just don't have those temperatures in my climate during spring. Once the nights warm and day temperatures get into the 80s (26°C), the cauliflower and broccoli heads move toward flowering (bolting). The head of a cauliflower is actually a mass of immature flower stalks. Broccoli falls into two basic categories; the first is the heading variety that forms a large solid head at the center of the plant (this is the type of broccoli we're used to seeing). The second is a sprouting variety that forms smaller heads across the entire plant. These heads are called "florets," and like cauliflower, when the warm temperatures and soil arrive with regularity, they go to flower.

Cauliflower and broccoli need a good sixty to eighty days from transplant to produce the nice-sized heads we're accustomed to. Through trial and error, and using my journal, I learned the springs in my area just warmed too quickly. I now know to plant these in early August and pick them in fall. However, I still plant cauliflower and broccoli in spring because the entire plant is edible for the most part. I love harvesting the leaves for salads. They're full of vitamins and a perfect source of minerals in our diets. The smaller heads are delicious too. Recently, I start growing the sprouting variety of broccoli and it seems to do better. It's a good lesson: Not all plant types will do well in your homestead garden. Make notes and keep trying new varieties. As you plant and grow, keep in mind that plants can be started during different points of the year.

Growing Cauliflower and Broccoli

Crop Type: Cool-Season

Average Soil Planting Temperature: 40°F to 50°F (4°C to 10°C)

Transplants: Start 6 weeks before planting them outdoors.

Direct Seeding: Plant 2 seeds per hole ½ inch (1 cm) deep. Cover and water them in well. Thin seedlings to 1 plant when plants are 2 inches (5 cm) tall.

Plant Spacing: 1 foot (30 cm) apart and 18 inches (45 cm) between rows

Growing Tips: Increase spacing for larger heads. Direct sow in midsummer for a fall crop 90 days before your average fall frost date.

Container Tips: Grow 1 plant per 5- to 10-gallon (19 to 38 L) container. Keep soil moist and fertilize every 2 weeks with a water-soluble fertilizer.

kale and collard greens

I consider kale the ultimate four-season crop because many varieties can withstand winters with regularly freezing nights. I plant kale in spring and let it go. This vegetable tastes and grows its best during the cool seasons. I eat the leaves in late spring, summer, and through fall; the leaves are sweeter and taste best in salads when it's cool. Come summer, the leaf flavor changes, and I tend to cook them more with potatoes and other dishes. They don't produce much during winter, but they often survive, and come spring, they flower for the pollinators. Kale plants are biennial, which means they grow and establish for one year and the next year they flower. When they flower, they stop producing leaves, but you'll get tiny flower buds and yellow flowers, which are delicious and make great salad additions. Kale is one of the easiest plants from which to collect seed after it flowers. They produce hundreds of long pods, and a single plant can produce over a thousand seeds. Seed collecting is one way to lower the costs on your homestead. They certainly can be used for your garden but can also be traded and sold. Bartering with goods from your garden is a great way to build community.

Several years ago, I had a good laugh when everyone was talking about the new superfood called "kale." Of course, kale popped up everywhere commercially as if it were a new discovery. Kale has been grown for centuries, but when we become accustomed to walking into a grocery and buying what is available, we miss out on standards that have fed people from the gardens for centuries. It may be a superfood, but kale is not new.

Kale is a must for any homestead garden because of its versatility, taste, and nutritional value. Varieties of kale I grow every year are 'Red Russian', 'Blue Curled Scotch', and 'Lacinato'.

Growing Kale and Collard Greens

Crop Type: Cool-Season

Average Soil Planting Temperature: 40°F to 50°F (4°C to 10°C)

Transplants: Start 6 weeks before planting them outdoors.

Direct Seeding: Plant 2 seeds per hole ½ inch (1 cm) deep. Cover and water them in well. Thin seedlings to 1 plant when plants are 2 inches (5 cm) tall.

Plant Spacing: 1 foot (30 cm) apart and 12 to 18 inches (30 to 45 cm) between rows

Growing Tips: Spray every 2 weeks with Neem oil to manage caterpillars.

Container Tips: Grow 1 plant per 5- to 10-gallon (19 to 38 L) container. Fertilize every 2 weeks with a water-soluble fertilizer.

Collard greens are very similar to kale but have larger flat leaves. You grow them the same way, and the flavor and nutrition mirror kale. I recommend growing a variety or two of collards; I always grow 'Georgia Southern'. Collards are biennials but they can easily be confused with kale when planted early in spring. They seem to need less of a cold period than kale to initiate flowering. Therefore, they may bolt during the warm period.

cabbages

Cabbage is another cool-season crop, thriving when day-time temperatures remain in a range of 55°F to 75°F (13°C to 24°C).

Cabbage leaves are sweet during cool weather and can become spicy in warm weather. There are heading varieties and leaf varieties. Heading varieties can be stored for a good period, making them a great crop for homesteaders who want to eat their homegrown harvest well into winter. Leaf varieties should be used within a few days after being picked. I always grow 'Early Jersey Wakefield' as it matures early, at sixty-five days. That works well for my spring and fall temperatures. The weight of a cabbage head can vary from as low as 2 pounds (910 gm) up to 50 pounds (23 kg) with some record-setting cabbages weighing over 100 pounds (45.5 kg). This, of course, is based on seed variety and temperatures during the growing period. Cabbages are heavy feeders as you might have gathered from heads that can weigh 50 pounds (23 kg).

Growing Cabbage

Crop Type: Cool-Season

Average Soil Planting Temperature: 40°F to 50°F (4°C to 10°C)

Transplants: Start 6 weeks before planting them outdoors.

Direct Seeding: Plant 2 seeds per hole ½ inch (1 cm) deep. Cover and water them in well. Thin seedlings to 1 plant when plants are 2 inches (5 cm) tall.

Plant Spacing: 18 to 24 inches (45 to 60 cm) apart and 2 feet (60 cm) between rows

Growing Tips: Direct sow in midsummer for a fall crop 90 days before your area's average fall frost date.

Container Tips: I don't recommend them for containers.

radishes

I have a fondness for radishes and struggled to grow them for years. I grew great leaves but harvested few radishes. It turns out, I was overpreparing the soil with nitrogen fertilizers and feeding them too much. Neglect radishes except for consistent watering, and you'll have a great harvest. Don't fertilizer the bed with anything more than yearly compost. This took me years to figure out; I learn new things every year. Radishes are grown for their bulbous root, and any excess love you give them seems to go right to the leaves.

The classic 'French Breakfast' radish can be ready to harvest in as little as twenty-five days from germination.

My favorite yearly standard radish is a hybrid called 'Roxanne'. It is a steady producer of red, golf-ball-sized radishes. While most plants can be grown from transplants, radish seeds should be directly sown into the garden early in spring. Space seeds so you'll have at least 1 inch (2.5 cm) between the bulbous roots at maturity. Overcrowded radishes produce underwhelming radish bulbs.

Since radishes mature quickly, plant them is succession. Succession planting is a fancy way of saying "stagger" the planting times of a crop. If you sow one hundred radish seeds on the same day, in thirty days you will have about ninety radishes to eat in a single week and very few after that. Radishes are best sown in succession every two weeks. If your cool-weather growing period is ninety days, sow up to six plantings of radishes. That translates to planting a couple rows every two weeks up into the last weeks of your cool period. The key takeaways for a successful radish garden are: no extra fertilizer, proper spacing, and staggered plantings.

Radishes come in all different sizes and shapes. Some include the white-tipped, oblong 'French Breakfast'; the white-tipped, round 'Sparkler'; the long white radish called 'Icicle'; and 'Crimson Giant', a large, dark, round red radish. The long (carrotlike) red radishes of 'Red Daikon' or 'Long Scarlet' are other choices. 'Hailstone' is a white globe radish. There's even 'Watermelon', which has a white exterior and brilliant magenta center. Radishes are best grown during the cool season as the cool air tempers a radish's spiciness with sweetness. As it warms, the radish bulb becomes woody, and the plant bolts to produce seed. I grow them in spring and fall.

Growing Radishes

Crop Type: Cool-Season

Average Soil Planting Temperature: 40°F to 50°F (4°C to 10°C)

Transplants: I recommend direct seeding.

Direct Seeding: Plant 1 seed per hole ½ inch (1 cm) deep. Cover and water them in well.

Plant Spacing: 2 to 4 inches (5 to 10 cm) apart and 6 to 12 inches (15 to 30 cm) between rows

Growing Tips: Direct sow in late summer for a fall crop.

Container Tips: Grow them in flower boxes with a 4 to 6 inch (10 to 15 cm) depth.

asparagus

Asparagus isn't a standard cool-weather crop. It is actually a perennial plant that's harvested in spring when new shoots, or spears, emerge. Asparagus plants survive freezing temperatures, and, in fact, need a yearly dormancy period of cold. If you get a cold period that kills top growth, there's a good chance asparagus will do wonderfully in your homestead garden.

Asparagus can be grown from seed or crowns. I start asparagus seeds indoors about twelve weeks before I plant it out in the garden. The goal is to grow a great set of roots indoors so they take hold nicely once moved outdoors. Asparagus is harvested about two to three years after planting. If you don't want to start seeds, you can purchase one-year-old dormant crowns. Plant asparagus crowns or transplants 4 to 6 inches (10 to 15 cm) deep and space 12 to 18 inches (30 to 45 cm) apart. Let them

grow the first year without harvesting. Asparagus spears will grow very tall with very fine, ferny leaves. They look very different from the spears we eat. Let them grow all season and then cut the ferns back after they brown from frost and cold weather.

Asparagus spears are typically the first crop harvested in spring. I recommend planting a long row with twenty to twenty-five plants. If you want multiple rows, space them 3 feet (90 cm) apart. Spears are harvested at 6 to 8 inches (15 to 20 cm) tall over a two- to three-week period. You don't want to take all the spears from the root system because some have to be left to grow and replenish the plant. While you have to wait two to three years before a decent harvest, the beauty of this perennial crop is that it will produce for a good fifteen to twenty years.

onions

Even if you fail growing large onion bulbs, you'll still get delicious green growth you can use in salads, soups, and other dishes. Onion varieties fall into three main growing categories: short-day, intermediate-day (or neutral-day), and long-day. This is based on the length of daylight required to trigger bulb set. The most important thing to understand is that onion bulbing is not fully based on a period of growth. That's important, but it's length of daylight that triggers bulb formation. You are matching the onions you choose to grow to the length of daylight hours during your summers. This amount varies based on your geographical location.

Onion Day Length and Planting

Short-Day
10–12 hours of daylight
Spring planting
Matures in 75–90 days

Intermediate-Day or Neutral-Day
12–14 hours of daylight
Spring planting
Matures in 90–110 days

Long-Day
14–16 hours of daylight
Early spring planting
Matures in 90–110 days

Onion seeds will typically state on the package what type of onion they are. I plant mine in spring; where there are mild winters, you can also plant onions in fall. Essentially, I grow my own onion transplants, but you can buy onion seedlings in "bunches" of fifty, seventy-five, or one hundred. I recommend growing your own or purchasing transplant bunches because they bulb and mature better than the planting onion bulbs or sets.

You can also buy tiny onion bulbs or sets as another planting option. Onions are biennial plants. That means the first year they grow and bulb and produce what we like to harvest and eat. The second year, they flower and produce seed and forego significant bulb production.

Growing Onions

Crop Type: Cool-Season

Average Soil Planting Temperature: 40°F to 50°F (4°C to 10°C)

Transplants: Start 6 weeks before planting them outdoors.

Direct Seeding: Plant 1 seed per hole ½ inch (1 cm) deep. Cover and water them in well.

Plant Spacing: 4 to 6 inches (10 to 15 cm) apart and 6 to 12 inches (15 to 30 cm) between rows

Growing Tips: Prepare the planting area using bonemeal as directed on the packaging.

Container Tips: Plant seeds or transplants 4 inches (10 cm) apart and allow 2 inches (5 cm) of space between sides. Any size container can be used as long as it has a minimum of 6 inches (15 cm) of soil. You can plant them closer for smaller bulbs or to grow delicious greens.

lettuces

Lettuce can be a heading variety, such as 'Iceberg' or as loose-leaf lettuce, which basically means it doesn't form a head. I only grow loose-leaf lettuces. They come in so many different colors and textures. I prefer a leaf that's a little more rigid and can hold a dressing. Lettuce leaves are 90 percent water and really don't have a lot of nutritional value; that's why we grow a diversity of leafy greens. We can add the wonderful, peppery taste of arugula, the nutritious leaves of spinach, the spice of mustard greens, crunchy Swiss chard, and so many more. I even grow beets just for their leaves. A nice mix of greens is arugula combined with different varieties of colorful loose-leaf lettuce such as 'Salad Bowl Red', 'Black Seeded Simpson', 'Ruby', and a Romaine variety. I add some spinach and mustard greens and have plenty of greens for salads.

Lettuce leaves can freeze through during cold snaps, as can most greens, but they have an interesting cell structure that doesn't rupture when frozen like pepper and tomato leaves do. Therefore, lettuce leaves can freeze solid at night and defrost the next day. Lettuces will die when the freezes are cold enough to reach their roots.

I also enjoy leaf lettuces because you can harvest them as baby greens or let them fully mature. Don't pull

the roots out when you harvest loose-leaf lettuce at any size. Just pinch or snip off leaves you want by cutting them off at the ground. Leaving the roots intact will allow new leaves to grow, and you can get two or three harvests. Since greens are all about leaf production, nitrogen can really help encourage large harvests. A steady supply of a water-soluble organic fertilizer, every two weeks, leads to early and frequent harvests.

I start seeds indoors to get some transplants out early since seeds are slow to germinate if directly sown into the garden when the soil is cold. About four weeks after starting lettuces indoors, I direct sow more lettuce seeds in two different ways.

1. If you want to grow full-sized lettuce heads, place one seed per hole and space the plants 6 to 12 inches (15 to 30 cm) apart, depending on how large the mature plant gets.

2. If you want to grow cut-and-come-again baby lettuce, plant seeds in a long row about 1 inch (2.5 cm) apart.

One tip that helps manage snails and slugs is to leave about 6 inches (15 cm) between the lettuce rows when planting them densely together. Birds and toads will enjoy the space to glean the tasty snails and slugs.

Growing Lettuce

Crop Type: Cool-Season

Average Soil Planting Temperature: 40°F to 50°F (4°C to 10°C)

Transplants: Start 4 weeks before planting them outdoors.

Direct Seeding: Plant 1 seed per hole ½ inch (1 cm) deep. Cover and water them in well.

Plant Spacing: 2 to 4 inches (5 to 10 cm) for cut-and-come-again lettuces or 6 to 12 inches (15 to 30 cm) for mature heads.

Growing Tips: Direct seed in late summer for a fall harvest.

Container Tips: Grow them in flower boxes with a 4- to 6-inch (10 to 15 cm) depth.

YOUR FIRST GARDEN

My First Garden Crop Suggestions	Cool-Season 1	Warm-Season	Cool-Season 2	Suggested Varieties (Pick One)
Loose-Leaf Lettuce	X		X	'Salad Bowl Red', 'Bibb', 'Black Seeded Simpson'
Spinach	X		X	'Bloomsdale Long Standing'
Kale	X			'Red Russian', 'Scotch Blue Curled'
Radish	X		X	'French Breakfast', 'Roxanne', 'Cherry Belle'
Cabbage	X		X	'Early Jersey Wakefield', 'Red Acre'
Bunching Onions	X		X	'White Lisbon'
Cherry Tomato		X		Your choice
6- to 10-ounce Tomato		X		'Homestead', 'Marglobe', 'Rutgers'
16 ounces or more Tomato		X		'Mortgage Lifter', 'Big Zac'
Colored Tomato		X		'Green Zebra', 'Cherokee Purple', 'Jubilee Orange'
Hot Pepper One		X		Jalapeño, Red Cayenne, Facing Heaven
Hot Pepper Two		X		Poblano (Ancho), Anaheim Chilli
Sweet Pepper One		X		Sweet Banana, Cubanelle
Sweet Pepper Two		X		Any green bell pepper variety
Sweet Pepper Three		X		Any red, yellow, orange, or purple variety
Zucchini		X		'Black Beauty', 'Cocozelle'
Pickling Cucumber		X		'National Pickling'
Standard Cucumber		X		'Straight Eight', 'Marketmore'

These varieties are just suggestions. I have grown them all. This is a nice mix of standard vegetables to get you growing on your homestead.

There are so many other plants you can add to your garden in addition to those I just presented. There is nothing wrong with starting with the standards and adding other warm-season crops, such as eggplant, tomatillos, and okra, later.

It is so important to learn by doing, take notes, and move at a pace you enjoy. Before you know it, you'll have twenty-five different types of food crops in your garden and dozens of different varieties of tomatoes, peppers, cucumbers, and squash. In the next chapter, we'll talk about the basic set-up for starting seeds indoors and growing our own transplants.

3

SEEDS,
SEED-STARTING,
AND TRANSPLANTS

I **LOVE BUYING VEGETABLE SEEDS.** Of course, you can buy them anytime, but it is just one of those things I love doing in December and January as I wait for spring. It is a lot of fun and there are hundreds, if not thousands, of places to buy seeds. Search the internet for companies that offer free seed catalogs and sign up. Before you know it, you'll have dozens of beautiful color catalogs coming to your mailbox. You can certainly find seeds in stores but often you'll find the same seeds and varieties over and over again. Shopping for seeds online will open the door to thousands of different plant varieties that you can plant successfully in your homestead garden. Very often these are vegetables you can't find in grocery stores. You're no longer trapped into eating the same things. Seed buying is fun and even addictive. Consider this your fair warning.

Seed Terminology

Right away you're going to be hit with four terms when buying seeds. You will see non-GMO seeds, heirloom seeds, hybrid seeds, and organic seeds. Let me start by defining each of these terms.

GMO stands for *genetically modified organism*. You will never find GMOs in a retail seed packet. GMO seeds are big business, and they are available only to commercial farmers. You'd have to buy a small fortune's worth of seeds and sign contracts to be able to use them. They're used for large-scale farming. So don't worry about that and don't pay more just because a seed pack says non-GMO. All retail seed packs are non-GMO.

Heirloom seeds are plants that are stable cultivars. That means, if you save and collect the seeds and plant them the following year, you will get the same plant as the parent. Generally speaking, the plant variety that you're growing has to be at least fifty years old before it's considered an heirloom.

Hybrid seeds are made from crossing the genes of one plant variety with another plant variety. This occurs naturally in nature when bees and pollinating insects move pollen from plant to plant; it's a

---

The Modern Homestead Garden Mantra

Take a moment to give yourself credit for making a decision to learn and change. There's a lot to learn, and it can be overwhelming. As I cover the basic principles for building a homestead garden, remember to use them as guidelines instead of rules. All you need today to begin building your homestead garden is your desire and interest to learn. It's as much of a change in mindset as it's a labor of love. It's also work. Making the shift from being a full-time consumer to learning how to be more self-sufficient is admirable. It is as important to look at what you have accomplished as it is to think about what you have to do next.

natural process. It's also something plant breeders love to do by hand.

People can spend decades creating their own hybrids. They do this out of a passionate desire to create a new plant variety that has new characteristics that meet specific needs such as better disease resistance, sweeter fruit, or better tolerance to heat or cold. If it weren't for the passion of plant breeders, how else would you be able to grow a 5-pound (2.27 kg) tomato? Or eat the amazingly sweet orange cherry tomato? Hybrid plant seeds differ from heirloom seeds because they are not stable cultivars. If you save the seeds of hybrids and plant them the following season, you won't necessarily get the same plant. It takes many generations of hybridizing before a plant becomes a stable cultivar.

Organic seeds can be confusing for gardeners. All seeds are pretty much organic, unless they are coated in a fungicide or other chemicals. When this is done, the chemical coating is often noticeably colored. The packets are typically marked as "treated" seeds. Otherwise, what really makes a seed organic? What could possibly be in tiny

tomato seed that is harmful to you? In my opinion, seeds marked "organic" are no better than seeds not marked "organic." Organic seeds were grown using certified organic growing methods; that's the main difference. And seeds that aren't marked organic, unless they're covered in colorful fungicide, are and have always been organic, though they weren't necessarily grown using certified organic practices. What you buy is your choice; I just want you to be informed.

Why Start Seeds Indoors

I really love starting most of my herbs, vegetables, flowers, and even fruits indoors from seeds. Not only does it save you a lot of money, it gives you access to just about every plant variety on the planet. Now, you might have to seek out unique plant varieties, but you can find them. Learning how to start your own seeds, propagate plants, and collect seeds add to your skill set to be more self-sufficient. As you become proficient in these skills, you can make extra money by having a vegetable plant yard sale or by selling them at flea markets. You can even use your transplants to barter with others. Trading garden plants and flowers for goat manure or fresh eggs is something I have done.

Seeds are started indoors primarily as a way to have healthy mature transplants that go out into the garden when the temperatures are right. By doing this, your plants

mature more quickly and your homestead harvests start sooner.

If you live in a place with a shorter growing season, seed-starting indoors is a skill to learn. Growing transplants indoors allow plants to grow for four, six, eight, or more weeks, giving your plants a significant head start before they are planted outside. This allows you to get a jump on the growing season. Planting seeds directly into the garden works but the unpredictability of rain, cold temperatures, and even pests can delay germination and harm young plants so much that you have to seed again. Growing indoors allows you to control the immediate environment and grow strong transplants. In regions with a short growing season, you can grow plants to full maturity that otherwise would not have enough time to mature when sown by seed. A tomato plant started indoors will produce ripe tomatoes more quickly than a seed planted in the ground on the same day as the transplant was planted. Maximizing garden production is a goal of any homestead garden.

THE BENEFITS OF STARTING SEEDS INDOORS

- It's a lot of fun.

- It gives your garden a jump on the growing season, and you can get food more quickly to your table.

- If you have a short growing season, it allows you to grow plants you could not otherwise grow.

- Nursery-bought transplants are expensive. Growing your own can cost pennies a plant.

- You have more choices in what you can grow and aren't stuck with the same old standard varieties sold at stores.

- You can sell extra transplants and use them to barter.

Plant Yard Sales and Flea Markets

Transplants can be expensive, and the varieties available are often limited. Once you're able to start seeds indoors, it isn't much more work to grow additional plants for a sale. People love tomatoes, peppers, cucumbers, squash, zucchini, kale, and herbs. Grow additional plants and sell them at half the price at which they are typically sold in local markets. Advertise to family and friends, through social media, and put up plant yard sale signs. If your plant yard sale goes well, look for local flea markets. You can use the extra income for garden projects and buying supplies.

How to Sterilize Seed-Starting Mix

Occasionally, a seed-starting mix may contain fungus gnat eggs. Fungus gnats are a problem you want to prevent rather than try to manage after they arrive. The eggs can remain dormant for long periods. Rather than roll the dice, boil water and fully saturate your seed-starting mix with it. You have to hydrate the starting mix anyway before planting, so using boiling water for the job performs two tasks in one. Turn the mix with a wooden spoon until it is steaming and fully hydrated. Starting mix dries out quickly, so if you are in doubt, add more boiling water to the mix. Once it's mixed, carefully press and pack down the mix to hold in the heat. I use a very large bowl to sterilize my seed-starting mix. Cover the top of the mix with aluminum foil to keep the heat in. Leave it alone until it is fully cooled.

How to Start Seeds Indoors

Starting seeds indoors is a fairly straightforward process, but you do need the right equipment for the job.

SEED-STARTING MIX

Start seeds in a sterile seed-starting mix. If you bring garden soil inside, even compost, you'll have problems. Outdoor soil has insects, insect eggs, fungi, and molds. The warmth of the house and from grow-lights support insect, mold, and fungal growth. These are problems you don't want and can avoid. Commercial seed-starting mixes purchased in sealed bags from a nursery may be sterile, but if you make your own mix or you question the integrity of a commercial mix, I recommend sterilizing it with boiling water before using.

MAKE YOUR OWN SEED-STARTING AND POTTING MIXES

Seed-starting mix is typically made with peat moss and vermiculite as the main ingredients. Sometimes perlite is added, but more often, it's used in general potting mixes. Buying premade mixes can be expensive when you're starting a lot of seeds or when you have to pot up many plants into larger containers. It may feel as if you're initially spending more money to buy the materials in bulk to make your own mixes, but it can be cheaper by 50 percent or more compared to the cost of the premade mixes.

Over the years, I changed the recipe for better germination and to keep the cost as low as possible. My favorite "recipe" consists only of peat moss and vermiculite. I no longer use perlite, but I include it in some of these recipes because some people feel it helps. I also add coco coir as an alternative to peat moss. However, I found seed germination was poorer when coco coir fully replaces peat moss. I did a side-by-side comparison, and the germination rate for a coco coir-and-vermiculate-filled flat was lower. Coco coir, however, is a renewable resource, unlike peat moss. A good alternative to using 6 parts peat moss is using 3 parts peat moss and 3 parts coco coir. The downside is that coco coir can be harder to find in bulk, in fine form, and it's more expensive than peat moss.

Peat moss is mined from peat bogs and many European bogs have been destroyed by exhaustive mining over the centuries. Canadian peat bogs are mined using better practices which includes restoring the bogs. However, it still takes generations for restored bogs to begin to reform the ecosystem needed to create peat moss. Whether it is effective is still debated. Coco coir, on the other hand, is made from the husks of coconuts that grow year after year. It is sustainable and renewable, meaning coco coir can be harvested without concern of permanently harming the ecosystem. These are ethical issues to consider when using products on your homestead.

The following recipe table is based on equal parts, which means use the same size container for measuring each ingredient.

SEED-STARTING MIX RECIPES

Peat Moss	Vermiculite (Fine Particles)	Perlite	Coco Coir (Fine Particles)	Notes
6	1	0	0	My favorite mix for starting seeds and general potting
6	1	1	0	A standard mix
0	1	0	6	A peat moss alternative
3	1	0	3	Another alternative
3	1	1	3	For gardeners who like the benefits of perlite

The key to success in seed starting is preventing problems, just like it is when tending a garden. Getting your seedlings off to a good start with the right seed-starting mix is essential.

SEED-STARTING FLATS, TRAYS, CELL PACKS, AND CONTAINERS

Based on the number of plants you plan to start indoors, you can get an idea of how many trays, seed-starting cells, and containers you will need. I easily start 750 or more

vegetable, flower, and herb plants indoors over a season, but you can start with a single nursery tray (called a "flat") filled with planting cell packs, which holds 72 plants. That is enough for a small garden. If you don't have access to a nursery flat, use foil oven pans or old baking sheets. These flats/trays hold the seed-starting cells, and they make it easy to move the plants around and water them.

Starting cells is the method typically used to germinate seeds and grow young transplants. Fill the cells with seed-starting mix and plant the seeds. The typical cell pack has six pockets for seeds; twelve cell packs fit into a standard nursery flat; twelve cells x six pockets equal seventy-two plants in each flat. But the pockets in a standard

6-cell pack are small. Some plant varieties quickly outgrow these small cells and have to be potted up into larger containers such as a 3- or 4-inch (7.5 or 10 cm) pots, plastic cups, or peat pots. When the transplants outgrow the cell, pop them out and pot them up into bigger containers. The larger containers will support most plants until they're ready to go out in the garden. If you aren't starting a lot of plants at once, then you can start your seeds directly in the larger containers and skip using the smaller starting cells.

GROW LIGHT BASICS

I don't recommend using a window for starting seeds. On the surface, it makes sense because sun shines into the window. However, there's rarely enough light for growing transplants, even in the brightest windows. Seeds will germinate, but the seedlings won't thrive. Seedlings need intense light levels for fourteen to sixteen hours a day. Seedlings on a windowsill get indirect light. Instead of leafing out and becoming strong, stocky seed starts, the seedlings put all their energy into growing up toward the light. In doing this, they become tall, thin, and frail. This response is called "legginess," and it can be prevented by using proper lighting.

The lighting options on the market can be overwhelming. The first rule is to know what you are buying and realize you'll pay more for a lighting system packaged and labeled as a "grow light." Why not make your own lighting set-up instead? It's surprisingly easy. By simply buying the correct fluorescent tubes or LED lights, available at any hardware store or online, you'll save money while still getting seeds off to a great start.

What Kind of Light Bulb Is Needed?

Keep in mind we are growing transplants, not flowering and fruiting plants. The correct light intensity and wavelengths are all that're needed to start seeds and grow healthy transplants. There's no need to buy specialized grow lights or LED lights that are red, blue, and other colors. They work, but they can be more expensive and are really only needed if you want to encourage plants to flower indoors (such as when growing orchids or African violets).

The key to growing under lights is intensity, which is measured in lumens, and the wavelength/color of the light, which is measured in Kelvin. The lumen value should be a minimum of 2,000 lumens. With LED lights, you can achieve 5,000 lumens and much higher. A range of 2,000 to 5,000 lumens is perfect for seed-starting. For Kelvin, you want a range of 5,000 to 6,500, which mimics natural daylight.

When the measurements of your bulbs are on the lower end of these ranges, you have to keep the lights closer to your seedlings and leave them on for longer periods. When you look for lights to build your own seed-starting set-up, you'll find they vary greatly. Here are my basic guidelines for the ratings, which should help you wade through all the different lights you come across.

Basic Set-up for an Indoor Grow-Light Station

1. Purchase two sets of 4-foot-long (1.2 m) fluorescent shop lights.

2. Purchase a shelving unit and hang lights on the undersides of the shelves.

3. Purchase a timer to set the operation time for the lights automatically.

4. Set plants under the lights for sixteen hours a day to start and twelve to fourteen hours a day when the seedlings are ten to fourteen days old.

5. Your set-up should allow you to adjust the height of the lights on chains as the plants grow.

6. Another option for small scale lighting includes a table-top system built from PVC pipes and a single shop light.

SELECTING THE RIGHT LIGHTS

| Lumens = Light Intensity | | Range 2000–5000+ Lumens |
| Kelvin = Wavelength/Color of Light | | Range 5000–6500 Kelvin |
Lumens	Kelvin	Overall
1,750–2,000	5,000–6,500	Fair; light may need to be closer to plants.
2,000–4,000	6,000–6,500	Good; lights can sit 3 inches (7.5 cm) above plants.
4,000+	6,500K	Great; lights can sit higher above plants.

Four-foot-long (1.2 m) shop light fixtures hold two light tubes. You can choose to use standard LED tubes or fluorescent tubes. I found no significant difference between LED and fluorescent tubes when it comes to seed-starting, as long as you follow the ranges for the lumens and Kelvin values. LEDs will typically have a higher lumens value, and that allows you to have greater distance between the lights and plants. Fluorescent tubes can be less expensive, but you have to keep them closer to the plants. Aside from those differences, use what's within your budget and available in your area.

The design and size of your grow-light station will vary based on the number of plants you decide to start and manage indoors. I built my grow light station on shelves that were 4 feet by 36 inches (1.2 m by 0.9 m). Each shelf holds two, 4-foot-long (1.2 m) light fixtures. The lights are hung in pairs beneath each shelf level. A shelf with four levels can hold three sets of grow lights.

How Long to Run the Lights

The following chart provides a general routine for how long to leave the lights on during different phases of growth. Make sure the lighting cycles start as soon as you plant your seeds. Seeds do not typically need light to germinate, but seeds need to be greeted by intense light as soon as they break the surface of the starting mix. Many people wait until germination to turn on lights as a way to save electricity costs. I recommend using a timer to turn your lights on and off. It is easy to forget to turn on your lights, and missing just a single day, when plants are newly germinated, will cause plants to become leggy.

RECOMMEND LIGHT CYCLES FOR INDOOR SEED-STARTING

Connect lights to a timer. Start timer when seeds are planted.			
Growth Stage	Hours On	Hours Off	Details
Pre-Germination	16	8	Seeds should germinate into light. Waiting to turn the lights on after germination can cause problems.
Post-Germination	16	8	Follow 16–8 for the next 10–14 days of growth
After 10–14 Days of Growth	12–14	10–12	If the light lumens rating is 4,000+, you can use 12 hours if desired.
After 4 Weeks of Growth	12	12	Mature plants can manage with less light.

As your plants get older and larger, they are less affected by drops in light intensity or duration. Start with my suggested routine, take notes, and make adjustments. Growing your own transplants is much easier than it may sound. Plants *want* to grow. If you're worried about getting started, err on the side of more light until you find a routine that works for you. This is another skill that's best learned by doing and gaining experience.

Even though you're spending money to buy supplies, in the long run you'll save a considerable amount money. Grow lights for example, will last 40, 50, or 60 thousand hours or more. That's like a decade's worth of intense light for seed-starting indoors. Buying transplants at nurseries and stores can quickly add up, but you can grow your own transplants for a fraction of the price of store-bought plants.

INDOOR SEED-STARTING TECHNIQUES, WATERING, AND FERTILIZING BASICS

In theory, you can start any seeds indoors, but not all of them need to be. There are many that prefer to be planted directly into the garden soil outdoors (called "direct seeding" or "direct sowing"). The following chart of seeds to start indoors is based on what I've started indoors myself and then transplanted outdoors with regular success. Plants that don't tend to transplant well are those that form edible roots or grow long taproots, such as parsnips, radishes, and carrots. In the past I had been told (and I believed) that beets and peas would not do well if started indoors, but I experimented. I found they transplant extremely well and have been starting them indoors for years. Use this table as a guide, and I encourage you to experiment.

WHERE TO START SEEDS

Indoors	Outdoors
Bean	Arugula
Beet	Bok Choi
Broccoli	Carrot
Brussels Sprouts	Corn
Cabbage	Garlic
Cauliflower	Radish
Collard Greens	Parsnip
Cucumber	Potato
Eggplant	Rutabaga
Kale	Turnips
Lettuce	
Mustard Greens	
Melon	
Okra	
Peas	
Pepper	
Pumpkin	
Spinach	
Swiss Chard	
Tomatillo	
Tomato	
Watermelon	

TIMING IS EVERYTHING

Many homestead gardeners wonder when they should be starting their seeds indoors. Though it certainly depends on the exact variety of the vegetable, plants typically like to be planted into soil that's at least 50°F (10°C) or more at night. There's no need to split hairs or get lost in details other than to know plants vary on what they like, but this is a safe soil temperature target. Use the date when the average soil temperature is 50°F (10°C) at night in your area as the starting point to figure out when to start seeds indoors. Remember: What matters is the temperature of the *soil*, not the air. To determine when to start your plants indoors, count back from that date. Tomatoes should be started six to eight weeks before they'd go in the ground. Where I live, the soil reaches 50°F (10°C) around May 7. Counting back six weeks before that date is March 24, and eight weeks before that date is March 10, so that's when I start my tomato seeds indoors.

As a rule of thumb, soil temperature follows the average ambient temperatures by about two weeks. When nighttime temperatures are mostly in the 50s (10s) and daytime temperatures reach the 50s and 60s (10s and 15s) regularly over a two-week period, your soil temperature is rising. Add in some warm rains, and you can be confident the plants are ready for the outdoors. You can find average night and day temperatures for your area on the internet or ask local gardeners when they feel the soil has warmed.

Frost Plan and Cloches for Warm-Season Plants

Frost can kill or damage warm-season transplants. Not only do you want to identify the date when soil temperature is 50ºF (10ºC), you want to make sure you plant them out into the garden only after your area's last average frost date has passed. For example, May 1 might be the average date your garden soil gets to the 50ºF (10ºC) mark, but frost might arrive as late as May 15 based on averages over the years. Even though you have an idea when frost in unlikely, it can still arrive. It's important to have a plan in place for a surprise frost. Glass vases from thrift stores make great cloches (protective coverings that are placed over plants) and are often inexpensive. I have a couple dozen and use them when evening frost is expected. I just pop them over my plants in late afternoon and take them off in the morning. They'll protect plants from surprise late frosts, and they can also be used if you want to push the envelope and put plants out early.

Preparing Planting Cells and Seed Depth

Regardless of which types of seeds you plant and when, the seed-starting mix should be moistened prior to sowing. Fill your seed-starting cells or containers with the mix and press it down, fill again, and lightly press it in. Starting mix is very loose by design, but you want a nice, solid starting base for your seed's root system to grow into.

I have done many experiments on the seed planting depth and, because the starting mix is so light and porous, the difference between a ¼- to ½-inch (0.6 to 1 cm) seed-planting depth is negligible. Some seeds may need to be planted on the

surface and pressed in, but not covered. The seed packet typically tells you if a particular seed needs light to germinate. Otherwise, I scratch small seeds into the surface with a popsicle stick and press them in. Examples of small seed sizes are oregano, thyme, rosemary, and lavender. Larger seeds, such as pumpkin, melon, squash, cucumber, and sunflower seeds, are pushed in ½ inch (1 cm) deep. Plant all other seeds about ¼ inch (0.6 cm) deep. The bottom line is they are going to germinate at most depths. Don't overthink it.

Watering Seedling Trays

I recommend watering young plants from the bottom. Fill the trays beneath the cell packs with water and let the seed-starting mix and roots soak it up from beneath

through the drainage holes. Watering varies, and the key is to watch the top of the starting mix in each cell. The starting mix will be dark brown when it's saturated with water, and it will become light brown when it's dry. Let the top of the starting mix dry for a day or two before watering again to help reduce the risk of fungal issues.

To water, fill the tray about one-quarter full of water (which is sometimes

How to Start Seeds Indoors: A Cheat Sheet

1. Fill containers with sterilized seed-starting mix and press the mix in well.

2. When planting seeds that require light for germination, firmly press the seed-starting mix down, drop seeds, and press seeds onto the mix without covering them.

3. When planting very tiny seeds, press the seed-starting mix down, drop seeds, scratch them into the surface, and gently press the mix down.

4. When planting small seeds, press the seed-starting mix down, drop seeds, and press them about ¼ inch (0.6 cm) into the seed-starting mix with a pencil. Cover seeds and gently press the seed mix down.

5. When planting large seeds, press the seed-starting mix down, drop seeds, and press them about ½ inch (1 cm) into the mix with a pencil. Cover seeds and gently press the seed mix down.

6. Water newly planted seeds from the bottom. Fill the seed flat about one quarter of the way and let the water wick up from the bottom. After 30 minutes, dump out any excess water.

7. Don't water from the top or use humidity domes as they can cause problems for germinating seeds and seedlings.

8. See lighting guide for instructions on how long to keep the lights on as the seedlings develop. When in doubt, 14 hours on and 10 hours off works.

9. Fertilize plants with a water-soluble fertilizer at a very low amounts of N-P-K. Use a very diluted feeding. Overfertilizing can harm seedlings. Feed them after 10 to 14 days of growth from germination and every 7 to 14 days after that.

10. Water seedlings when the top of the starting mix is dry and has turned a light brown color. Saturated starting mix is dark brown. Allow the top of the starting mix to remain dry for 1 to 2 days before bottom watering your plants.

mixed with water-soluble fertilizer, more on this later). Wait thirty minutes for the water to be absorbed into the starting mix. The top of the starting mix should become saturated and turn dark brown again. If water is still sitting in the tray after the mix is dark brown and saturated, dump it out; I keep a bucket in my grow room for this purpose. If the mix is not fully saturated, add more water to the tray. With practice, you'll get good at adding the right amount of water.

I don't recommend watering seed starts from above. It's messy, more time consuming, and puts plants at risk. Watering from above can splash seeds and starting mix around, spread fungal diseases, and knock newly sprouted plants down. I also don't recommend humidity domes. I've tried them and found they only seem to create nice conditions for molds and fungi to grow.

Fertilizing Seedlings

Your plants are growing in a fairly small amount of starting mix. Remember, it's sterile and there's no soil microbiology. Thus, you'll need to use a water-soluble fertilizer beginning around the time when the seedlings develop their second set of leaves.

Complete water-soluble fertilizers have nitrogen, phosphorous, and potassium along with other nutrients in a form your plant can immediately absorb and use. You want a water-soluble fertilizer with a very low N-P-K ratio (1-1-1, for example), as noted on its package. If you can't find one with low numbers, dilute one with a higher N-P-K ratio by using less than is recommended on the label. Instead of using 1 tablespoon (15 ml) per gallon (3.8 L) of water as most mixes suggest, use ¼ tablespoon (4 ml), for example. You can always add more fertilizer, but you can't remove it. Too much fertilizer can damage your transplants and make them look sickly. All too often our response to sickly plants is to give them more fertilizer, and we end up killing them with kindness.

Generally speaking, after about ten to fourteen days of growth, give your seedlings their first dose of fertilizer when you water. You can fertilize them lightly every seven to fourteen days thereafter. Because no rain is reaching your seedlings, excess fertilizer concentrates in the starting mix instead of being washed away. The root systems of the plants are confined and sit in the excess, leading to possible fertilizer "burn." More isn't better; it's easy to overdo it.

Seed-Starting Questions, Tips, and Things to Keep in Mind

- Some seeds require a process called "stratification," meaning they need a prolonged cold period of fourteen to twenty-eight days (sometimes longer) to break dormancy in order to germinate. You can place your seed packet in the refrigerator for several weeks. The cold breaks down an enzyme in the seed that inhibits germination. The need for this is typically noted on the seed packet, but most vegetables do not require stratification.

- Some seeds require soaking or scratching the seed coat in order to germinate. This is typically noted on the seed packet.

- Seeds generally germinate more quickly at 65°F to 75°F (18°C to 24°C). You can use a heating mat both to hasten and improve germination. Pepper seeds tend to like more warmth.

- Don't allow plant leaves to touch the grow lights. While lights are generally cool, damage can occur.

- Cool-weather vegetables like cooler temperatures for germination. They germinate very quickly at 65°F to 75°F (18°C to 24°C), but they can grow too fast and become leggy due to the warm temperatures. A cool garage works well for them.

- Pop your seedlings out of their containers when they seem to be outgrowing their cell pack pocket. If the roots are coiling tightly at the bottom, it is time to pot them up into larger containers.

- Transplants are not used to the sun's UV rays when they've been started and grown indoors. They have to go through a process called "acclimation" or "hardening off" over a seven- to ten-day period. That means they have to be slowly introduced to the sun, wind, and outdoor temperatures gradually for a few hours every day until they're outdoors full-time.

- Don't start plants and hold them in containers much beyond the recommended range. Plants grown too long indoors can begin to flower and fruit too early. Flowering and fruiting are something you want to happen outdoors in the ground, not indoors.

- Use seed-starting mix made from combinations of peat moss, coco coir, vermiculite, and/or perlite. This creates a soilless mix. Bringing outdoor soil indoors will also bring in fungi, insects, and other problems.

Direct Sowing

Seeds that don't need to be started indoors are sown out into the garden using a process called "direct seeding" or "direct sowing." Starting seeds outdoors is really about waiting for soil conditions to be right. Your garden bed or container soil should be fully thawed to allow good drainage. Seeds that sit in cold, soggy soil will rot. Peas are a good example because, as a cool-season crop, they are some of the first seeds to be sown outdoors. You can start sowing seeds outdoors when the soil drains well and it has warmed to about 45°F (7°C). This is what cool-season crops prefer on the lower end of nighttime ambient temperatures. The seeds of those varieties are what we typically sow first. Seeds of warm-season crops and flowers aren't sown until the danger of frost has passed and the soil temperature has warmed sufficiently. Now let's talk about seed and row spacing for seeds that are direct sown.

Leave it to fellow gardeners to make putting a seed in the ground more complicated than it needs to be. There are spacing guides everywhere, and they vary quite a bit. Use them as guidelines, and not rules; for one reason, there's no exact distance to space a seed or a row. Nature doesn't care about proper spacing, so don't get lost in those details. Seeds are designed to germinate, mature, and produce in all kinds of conditions. Seeding spacing will vary based on the planting method you follow. Ultimately, you'll develop a style that fits your unique homestead.

One planting method, called "intensive gardening," is all about planting seeds and crops very closely together to save space, crowd out weeds, and get more yields from less space. I really like this method. Then you have "square foot gardening," which is a notch below intensive gardening. This method is wonderful for saving space and maximizing yields too. I also like this method. Before both of those, basic planting guidelines allowed full mature plant growth and better management for tending. This method promotes more space between plants and a greater distance between rows. I agree with the benefits of this approach. They all have their place, and you can practice parts of all three approaches as you find your style.

On pages 72 to 73 is a chart of the more common vegetables planted from seed. I took the averages from several sources for seed and row spacings to create this chart. Those numbers may differ from my spacing suggestions in chapter 2. Please use this as a guide and basic starting point. The problem with using charts like this one is that they give us

information without knowing anything about *your* garden design. We rarely plant everything in long rows in our homestead gardens. I plant zucchini and summer squash tucked in corners of various beds. So available growing space, for each garden, varies greatly. We might be using a mix of earth beds and containers. Vertical gardening is more common (and something I recommend), and that changes plant spacing and row spacing too. Finally, seed and row spacings depend upon the diseases and pests you have in *your* garden. If you are plagued by whiteflies and armyworms, you probably don't want dense plantings of kale or collard greens.

HOW TO DIRECT SOW

Prepare the soil first. I prepare my earth beds and raised beds by adding 1 inch (2.5 cm) of manure or compost across the top of the planting area and turning and mixing it to a depth of 6 to 12 inches (15 to 30 cm) with a spade. The goal is to loosen the soil and distribute the manure and compost. If you don't have these amendments, use any granular organic fertilizer at a rate of 2 to 4 tablespoons (30 to 60 ml) per square foot. Mix it in the same way.

I use my finger to press a ½-inch (1 cm) hole into the soil, at various intervals based on the plant variety. I found this is a quick and simple way to sow seeds and set up the planting holes. For example, I'll make a row of twenty-four holes, ½ inch (1 cm) deep, 2 inches (5 cm) apart for radishes. I drop two seeds per each finger hole and cover. I thin them to one plant when the seedlings are about ½ inch (1 cm) tall, keeping the strongest one. For container planting, equally space the ½-inch (1 cm) holes in the container and drop the seeds in the hole. A ½-inch (1 cm) depth works for most seeds. Larger seeds such as beans can be pushed down farther to a depth of 1 inch (2.5 cm). After sowing seeds, water them in and water two to three times a week until they establish.

To refresh older container soil, I dump the soil mix onto a tarp. I add 4 to 6 tablespoons (60 to 90 ml) of any granular organic fertilizer that has nitrogen, phosphorous, *and* potassium per 5 gallons (19 L) worth of mix. I may add several handfuls of compost when I have it. I add a couple handfuls of peat moss or coco coir for added moisture retention, and I refill the containers. Again, use my method as a base to create your own method. You'll find more on container gardening in chapter 5.

GENERAL SPACING AND MINIMUM SOIL TEMPERATURE RECOMMENDATIONS

Vegetable	Plant Spacing Average (Inches)	Row Spacing Average (Inches)	Soil Temperature Range	Cool-Weather	Warm-Weather
Asparagus	12–18 (30–45 cm)	60 (1.5 m)	60°F–70°F (16°C–21°C)	X	
Beans, Bush	2–4 (5–10 cm)	18–24 (45–60 cm)	70°F–75°F (21°C–24°C)		X
Beans, Pole	4–6 (10–15 cm)	30–36 (76–90 cm)	70°F–75°F (21°C–24°C)		X
Beets	3–4 (7.5–10 cm)	12–18 (30–45 cm)	50°F–60°F (10°C–16°C)	X	
Broccoli	18–24 (45–60 cm)	36–40 (90–100 cm)	50°F–60°F (10°C–16°C)	X	
Brussels Sprouts	24 (60 cm)	24–36 (60–90 cm)	50°F–60°F (10°C–16°C)	X	
Cabbage	9–12 (23–30 cm)	36–44 (90–110 cm)	50°F–60°F (10°C–16°C)	X	
Carrot	1–2 (2.5–5 cm)	12–18 (30–45 cm)	50°F–60°F (10°C–16°C)	X	
Cauliflower	18–24 (45–60 cm)	18–24 (45–60 cm)	50°F–60°F (10°C–16°C)	X	
Corn	10–15 (26–38 cm)	36–42 (90–106 cm)	60°F–70°F (16°C–21°C)		X
Cucumber	2–4 (5–10 cm)	30 (76 cm)	60°F–70°F (16°C–21°C)		X
Collards	10–18 (26–45 cm)	36–42 (90–106 cm)	50°F–60°F (10°C–16°C)	X	
Eggplant	18–24 (45–60 cm)	30–36 (76–90 cm)	65°F–75°F (65°C–75°C)		X
Kale	10–18 (26–45 cm)	36–42 (90–106 cm)	50°F–60°F (10°C–16°C)	X	
Leeks	4–6 (10–15 cm)	8–16 (20–40 cm)	50°F–60°F (10°C–16°C)	X	
Lettuce, Head	12 (30 cm)	12 (30 cm)	50°F–60°F (10°C–16°C)	X	
Lettuce, Loose Leaf	1–3 (2.5–7.5 cm)	1–3 (2.5–7.5 cm)	50°F–60°F (10°C–16°C)	X	
Melon	24–36 (60–90 cm)	48–60 (120–152 cm)	65°F–75°F (18°C–24°C)		X

Vegetable	Plant Spacing Average (Inches)	Row Spacing Average (Inches)	Soil Temperature Range	Cool-Weather	Warm-Weather
Onion	4–6 (10–15 cm)	4–6 (10–15 cm)	60°F–70°F (16°C–21°C)	X	
Peas	1–2 (2.5–5 cm)	18–24 (45–60 cm)	50°F–60°F (10°C–16°C)	X	
Pepper	14–18 (35–45 cm)	18–24 (45–60 cm)	65°F–75°F (18°C–24°C)		X
Potato	8–12 (20–30 cm)	30–36 (76–90 cm)	50°F–60°F (10°C–16°C)	X	
Pumpkin	48–72 (1.2–1.8 m)	48–72 (1.2–1.8 m)	70°F–80°F (16°C–27°C)		X
Radish	1–4 (2.5–10 cm)	2–4 (5–10 cm)	50°F–60°F (10°C–16°C)	X	
Spinach	2–4 (5–10 cm)	12–18 (30–45 cm)	45°F–55°F (7°C–13°C)	X	
Squash, Summer	18–28 (45–71 cm)	36–48 (90–120 cm)	65°F–75°F (18°C–24°C)		X
Squash, Winter	24–36 (60–90 cm)	48–60 (120–152 cm)	65°F–75°F (18°C–24°C)		X
Swish Chard	6–12 (15–30 cm)	12–18 (30–45 cm)	50°F–60°F (10°C–16°C)	X	
Tomato	24–36 (60–90 cm)	36–48 (90–120 cm)	65°F–75°F (18°C–24°C)		X
Turnip	2–4 (5–10 cm)	12–18 (30–45 cm)	50°F–60°F (10°C–16°C)	X	
Zucchini	24–36 (60–90 cm)	36–48 (90–120 cm)	65°F–75°F (18°C–24°C)		X

DIRECT SOWING IN CONTAINERS

Keep seeds 1–2 inches (2.5–5 cm) from the container sides and space holes evenly.
Take notes on how your plants perform based on your choice of spacing.

Vegetable	Soil Temperature Range	5- to 10-Gallon (38 L) Container	10- to 20-Gallon (76 L) Container	½ Inch (1 cm) Deep	1 Inch (2.5 cm) Deep	Tips
Asparagus	60°F–70°F (16°C–21°C)	1 hole	1 hole		X	Plant 3 seeds and thin to 1 plant.
Bean, Bush	70°F–75°F (21°C–24°C)	2–4 holes	4–8 holes		X	Plant 1 seed per hole and replace seeds that don't germinate.
Bean, Pole	70°F–75°F (21°C–24°C)	2–3 holes	4–6 holes		X	Plant 1 seed per hole and replace seeds that don't germinate.
Beet	50°F–60°F (10°C–16°C)	6–8 holes	8–16 holes	X		Each beet seed is a pod that holds several seeds. Plant one pod and thin to 1 plant.
Broccoli	50°F–60°F (10°C–16°C)	1 hole	2 holes	X		Plant 2 seeds per hole and thin to 1 plant.
Brussels Sprouts	50°F–60°F (10°C–16°C)	1 hole	2 holes	X		Plant 2 seeds per hole and thin to 1 plant.
Cabbage	50°F–60°F (10°C–16°C)	1 hole	2 holes	X		Plant 2 seeds per hole and thin to 1 plant.
Carrot	50°F–60°F (10°C–16°C)	10–15 holes	15–30 holes	X		Place 2 seeds per hole and thin to 1 plant.
Cauliflower	50°F–60°F (10°C–16°C)	1 hole	2 holes	X		Plant 2 seeds per hole and thin to 1 plant.
Corn	60°F–70°F (16°C–21°C)	X	8 holes		X	Use a 20-gallon container. 1 seed per hole.
Cucumber	60°F–70°F (16°C–21°C)	1 hole	2–3 holes	X		Plant 2 seeds per hole and thin to 1 plant.
Collards	50°F–60°F (10°C–16°C)	1 hole	2 holes	X		Plant 2 seeds per hole and thin to 1 plant.
Eggplant	65°F–75°F (18°C–24°C)	1 hole	2 holes	X		Plant 2 seeds per hole and thin to 1 plant.
Kale	50°F–60°F (10°C–16°C)	1 hole	2 holes	X		Plant 2 seeds per hole and thin to 1 plant.
Leeks	50°F–60°F (10°C–16°C)	3–5 holes	6–10 holes	X		Plant 2 seeds per hole and thin to 1 plant.
Lettuce, Head	50°F–60°F (10°C–16°C)	1–2 holes	2–4 holes	X		Plant 2 seeds per hole and thin to 1 plant.
Lettuce, Loose Leaf	50°F–60°F (10°C–16°C)	3–5 holes	6–10 holes	X		Plant 2 seeds per hole and thin to 1 plant.
Melon	65°F–75°F (18°C–24°C)	X	1 hole		X	Plant 2 seeds per hole and thin to 1 plant.

Vegetable	Soil Temperature Range	5- to 10-Gallon (38 L) Container	10- to 20-Gallon (76 L) Container	½ Inch (1 cm) Deep	1 Inch (2.5 cm) Deep	Tips
Onion	60°F–70°F (16°C–21°C)	10–12 holes	20–24 holes	X		Plant 2 seeds per hole and thin to 1 plant.
Peas	50°F–60°F (10°C–16°C)	6–8 holes	12–16 holes		X	Plant 1 seed per hole and replace seeds that don't germinate.
Pepper	65°F–75°F (18°C–24°C)	1–2 holes	2–4 holes	X		Plant 2 seeds per hole and thin to 1 plant.
Potato	50°F–60°F (10°C–16°C)	2–3 holes	4–6 holes	n/a	n/a	Use seed potatoes and press them down 4–6 inches (10–15 cm) deep.
Pumpkin	70°F–80°F (21°C–27°C)	X	1 hole		X	Plant 2 seeds per hole and thin to 1 plant.
Radish	50°F–60°F (10°C–16°C)	12–16 holes	24–32 holes	X		Plant 2 seeds per hole and thin to 1 plant.
Spinach	45°F–55°F (7°C–13°C)	4–6 holes	8–12 holes	X		Plant 2 seeds per hole and thin to 1 plant.
Squash, Summer	65°F–75°F (18°C–24°C)	X	1 hole		X	Plant 2 seeds per hole and thin to 1 plant.
Squash, Winter	65°F–75°F (18°C–24°C)	X	1 hole		X	Plant 2 seeds per hole and thin to 1 plant.
Swish Chard	50°F–60°F (10°C–16°C)	2–3 holes	4–6 holes	X		Plant 2 seeds per hole and thin to 1 plant.
Tomato	65°F–75°F (18°C–24°C)	1 hole Determinate	1 hole Indeterminate	X		Plant 2 seeds per hole and thin to 1 plant.
Turnip	60°F–70°F (16°C–21°C)	6–8 holes	12–16 holes	X		Plant 2 seeds per hole and thin to 1 plant.
Zucchini	65°F–75°F (18°C–24°C)	X	1 hole		X	Plant 2 seeds per hole and thin to 1 plant.

Planting Your Transplants

As I've mentioned, plants grown indoors under grow lights do not have a tolerance for the sun's ultraviolet (UV) rays. They aren't used to the wind or fluctuating temperatures. If you put a flat of transplants you so proudly grew indoors for six to eight weeks, outdoors under the full sun for several hours, they will burn. You have to acclimate all indoor plants to the outdoor sun, wind, and temperatures slowly. This is called "hardening off," and it should be done over seven to ten days. I can't tell you an exact way to do it because any seven- to ten-day period will have different weather. But here's one method that I find useful: After your seeds germinate, expose them to 30 minutes of outdoor conditions twice weekly when the air temperature is above freezing. Do this as they grow and mature indoors. They will begin to build up UV tolerance and the hardening-off process will go much more smoothly.

A week to ten days before you're ready to move your transplants out in the garden permanently, introduce them to the sun and begin the hardening off process. Place transplants outside in full sun for 30 minutes the first day. If it's a fully cloudy day, you can put them out for 60 minutes. You may get some white patches on leaves during this process, and it's normal. (That's damage from the UV rays.) Each day after that, extend the time outdoors by 15 to 30 minutes. The hardening-off process is completed over a period of seven to ten days. Keep in mind that a sunny day is very different than a fully cloudy day; you may have to adjust your process based on the weather.

Once your plants are ready for the outdoors and the soil temperatures are correct, follow the same soil preparations you did for sowing seeds. You can further amend the immediate planting hole when placing the transplants in the ground. I sometimes add worm castings, lime, or other amendments and mix them in well into the bottom of the planting hole. Select the spacing you like best, dig a hole, and place your transplant into the hole to the same depth it was in its container or cell pack. Generally, the only vegetable you want to plant deeper is a tomato transplant. I bury one-third to one-half of a tomato's stem when placing it in a container or into the ground. Roots will quickly grow from the sides of its buried stem.

Now that you know the basic for planting your garden from seeds or transplants, let's discuss the continued care of your plants and homestead garden throughout the entire growing season, starting with fertilization.

4

FEEDING YOUR HOMESTEAD GARDEN

PLANTS NEED A SLOW, STEADY SUPPLY OF NUTRIENTS.

As plants grow, they take nutrients from the soil that need to be replenished. Compost, worm castings, organic fertilizers, and chemical fertilizers are different ways to add essential nutrients to your garden's soil. Not only do your plants need nutrients, they also have to be supported by the microbiology that make up soil life and feed on organic matter in the soil. Compost, worm castings, and organic fertilizers all feed your plants organically, but they don't necessarily take care of your soil equally.

Organic fertilizers, such as bloodmeal, bonemeal, fish emulsion, and pelletized chicken manure, provide some organic matter to the soil, but they mostly serve to feed the soil microbiology. Soil life eats and digests organic fertilizers and changes the insoluble forms of the nitrogen, phosphorous, and potassium fertilizer compounds into water-soluble forms your plants can immediately use. Organic fertilizers feed the soil life and, in turn, the soil life feeds your plants. Bagged and bottled organic fertilizers are great options, but they don't always add enough organic matter into the garden. Organic matter helps maintains soil structure and holds moisture in the soil.

Processed chemical fertilizers do a fine job of feeding your plants, though they don't feed soil life or contribute to building healthy soil. These fertilizers have their place and can be used minimally in your gardens, but they should not be used regularly. Overuse and abuse of these fertilizers on large-scale farming levels have led to well documented soil problems. These real problems have morphed into misinformation to make us feel like a single use of these fertilizers wipes out all our garden's soil life. That's simply not true. It's important to understand how they work and how you might choose to use them.

Insoluble vs. Soluble Fertilizers

As you know, there are many different kinds of fertilizers on the market. How do you know which ones are best for your homestead garden? Begin by understanding the differences between insoluble and soluble fertilizers.

Insoluble means not easily dissolved into water. Plants use water to pull in some of the elements they need from the soil. Generally, if what they need can't be dissolved into water, then it won't pass into their root system. It also means they can't easily absorb it through their leaves as a foliar feeding. Insoluble fertilizers are known as slow-release and are typically organic granular-type products. This means it will take time for them to break down into a soluble form when placed into garden soil. This's why soil microbes are so important. They digest insoluble compounds and basically change them into a water-soluble form plants can use. Organic granular fertilizers are used to slowly feed your plants over the season. The soil life will break them down a little bit each day. In general, insoluble means a slower release of nutrients.

Most organic granular fertilizers are made from the same materials, with the main ingredients being animal byproducts, mined minerals, manures, and plant-based products. Bloodmeal, which is an animal byproduct, is very high in nitrogen and is made from slaughterhouse animal blood. Bonemeal, another animal byproduct, is high in phosphorous and calcium and is made from crushed cattle bones. Plant-based ingredients include cottonseed meal, alfalfa meal, and kelp meal. In the end, plants don't care what product you buy as long as they get a steady supply of nutrients. Keep in mind, however, that good old compost is also a form of slow-release fertilizer. Don't get trapped into the game of using expensive organic fertilizers: think compost. When it comes to organic granular fertilizers, buy what you like but always pay a fair price. There's nothing magical in them that isn't in good old compost.

Soluble means easily dissolved in water. With soluble fertilizers, nitrogen, phosphorous, potassium, and other elements your plants need are in a chemical form that immediately mixes into water and is readily available to plants. Plants can absorb this fertilizer through their roots and often through their leaves, to some degree. Water-soluble fertilizers are considered fast-acting. You mix, pour, and your plant pulls the fertilizer into their system. Soil biology and microbes are not typically needed with water-soluble fertilizers. You can buy organic and processed chemical fertilizers that are water-soluble. The organic types are better as they don't harm or affect soil life. In fact, they can provide them with food. The chemical types are not toxic to us or our plants, but they do not provide anything for the soil. They can be used as needed on an emergency basis, such as if you have severe damage to your crops and want them to recover quickly. They can even be used several times over a season, if that's what you choose. If you solely rely on processed chemical fertilizers, year after year, that's when they can damage soil life. I stress this point because I want you to understand all things are chemicals. Processed chemical fertilizers are not a replacement for compost or organic fertilizers. However, they will not harm you, your plants, or soil microbiology with limited use.

The best way to provide a continuous supply of nutrients to garden soil and plants is to make and use your own compost. It's important to fertilize your plants, but it's equally important to feed the soil life that helps sustain optimum plant heath and growth. Healthy soil and soil life (worms, fungi, bacteria, and so on) mean happy, hardy plants. Compost does it all. It adds nutrients and organic matter. It also improves soil structure, creates better water retention during dry periods, and encourages better drainage during heavy rains. Compost is a win across the board.

Once your homestead garden is up and running, you will want to work on making your own compost.

Why Compost?

Self-sufficiency is built on utilizing materials that are local and often free. Making compost embodies those two points. Compost is best made from the free resources already found on your homestead.

Making your own compost removes your reliance on bagged and bottled fertilizers. It's the only way to adequately supply your garden with the organic matter it needs, on all levels, and sustain its ability to produce year after year. When we talk about fertilizing your homestead gardens, we're talking about feeding the plants *and* the soil. I'll offer more advice on how to make your own compost later in this chapter, but first, I'd like to share some information on plant nutrition.

Plant Nutrients

Let's start with a very basic understanding of how chemicals relate to plants and soil microbiology. First, let's dispel the myth that the word "chemical" is bad and harmful.

"Chemical" does not equate to toxic or poison. Everything on the planet is made up of chemical elements. There are over 100 different naturally occurring elements that make up the world as we know it. These elements can combine together to form chemical compounds. Water is a chemical compound made when the elements of hydrogen and oxygen combine to form a molecule. This is important because compost and organic fertilizer are also made from chemical elements. The creation and decay of life (organic matter) is a chemical process. This decay creates the composted materials our plants and soil love. Plant growth depends on soil microbes breaking down the chemical compounds found in decaying organic matter from leaves, wood, grass, and other sources. In brief, we feed the soil compost, and then microbes eat the organic

matter in that compost and break it down into a form of chemical elements the plants can use to grow and flourish. Chemical fertilizers that are created in a laboratory don't add any organic matter to the soil or feed the microbes, but they do provide nutrients. Many gardeners use them for container and hydroponic gardening where soil life is less important or nonexistent. Chemical fertilizers can be used in your garden, but whether or not you choose to use them is up to you.

HOW THE SIX MAIN ELEMENTS HELP PLANTS

	Function	Signs of Deficiency
Nitrogen (N)	Nitrogen is part of every protein in the plant. It's essential for plant growth and in fighting diseases. Nitrogen is part of the chlorophyll molecule that gives a plant leaf its green color.	Yellowing of leaves. Yellowing typically starts on the older lower leaves first. Plants may be stunted and grow slowly.
Phosphorous (P)	Phosphorous is involved in cell membrane development, metabolism, and energy transfer. Think of it as moving resource through the stem to the leaves. It is involved in root development, flowering, and fruit production.	Darkening or purpling of leaves. Plants may have smaller-looking leaves and look stunted.
Potassium (K)	Potassium helps plants manage water pressure, stress, and metabolism. It's also involved in root growth	Brown scorching of plant leaf tips and edges. This typically appears on lower leaves first.
Calcium (Ca)	Calcium is involved in a plant's ability to uptake other nutrients and for building strong cell walls. It's very important in overall plant growth.	Associated with blossom end rot and stunted plant growth and fruit development.
Sulfur (S)	Sulfur is present in amino acids and helps build plant proteins.	Chlorosis (yellowing) of plant leaves and slow growth.
Magnesium (Mg)	Magnesium is a key element in chlorophyll and promotes greens growth. One atom of Mg surrounded by four atoms of N makes up the central core of a chlorophyll molecule.	Yellowing of leaves across the plant and sometimes leaf tip curling.

PRIMARY GARDEN MACRONUTRIENTS

There are six main macronutrients—chemical elements—plants need at higher and more consistent levels, and they are divided into two categories. The primary or major macronutrients are nitrogen (N), phosphorus (P), and potassium (K). These elements are used in a greater quantity by plants, and they are the nutrients displayed on fertilizer packaging. When you buy fertilizer, you'll see a series of these three numbers on the bag or bottle indicating N-P-K.

Primary Macronutrients
(N) Nitrogen
(P) Phosphorous
(K) Potassium

Secondary Macronutrients
(Ca) Calcium
(S) Sulfur
(Mg) Magnesium

Micronutrients
(B) Boron
(Cl) Chloride
(Cu) Copper
(Fe) Iron
(Mn) Manganese
(Mo) Molybdenum
(Zn) Zinc

These numbers represent the amounts of nitrogen, phosphorus, and potassium, by percentage, inside a bottle or bag of fertilizer. A 5-4-3 fertilizer contains 5 percent nitrogen, 4 percent phosphorous, and 3 percent potassium. These are elements plants use in quantities higher than other nutrients.

SECONDARY GARDEN MACRONUTRIENTS

There are three secondary, or minor, macronutrients. Plants use these regularly but not in the same quantities as N, P, and K. These nutrients are essential to plant growth, so they need to be present in garden soil, but not in such large quantities. The secondary micronutrients are calcium (Ca), sulfur (S), and magnesium (Mg).

MICRONUTRIENTS, AKA TRACE ELEMENTS

There are also micronutrients (often called trace elements) that plants need, but they are needed at extremely low levels. Rarely, if ever, will you need to worry about trace elements in your garden soil. You can replace what's used by your garden with regular yearly applications of compost. Compost provides everything your plants and soil need to thrive.

As plants grow, they take from your garden soil. As plants die, they give back to the soil. However, unlike in a forest where leaves fall and decompose in place to return nutrients back to the soil, in a garden, nutrients are returned back to the soil

through composting. Composting leaves, grass clippings, weeds, old garden plants, and food scraps is a way to naturally and effectively return the macro- and micronutrients back to your soil. When you make compost, you're breaking organic matter down into its basic elemental form and returning it back to the soil. Composting is something we can all start to do immediately, even if it's only on a small scale. You don't have to feed your whole garden with it to start. Learning how to make and use compost is the first step to truly becoming self-sufficient.

Composting: Just Get Started

Composting is the ultimate way to fertilize garden plants, feed soil life, and build organic matter in your garden beds. It's also one of the best ways to become more self-sufficient and less dependent on purchased fertilizers or soil amendments. You can make you own, with some effort, and little out-of-pocket cost. The biggest barrier to getting started making compost is—getting started. We often feel we need to know how to do it perfectly. We hear that "hot composting" is the quickest way to make compost. However, composting is not a speed contest. Compost happens naturally as Nature is capable of doing this without our help. There are many ways to make compost, over short periods and long periods. The bottom line is, you just need to collect the resources and pile them up. Following are some basic guidelines that can help speed up the composting process.

Enjoy Your Homestead Journey

You share something special with fellow gardeners and homesteaders. I remember my third-grade science fair. I had a big poster that read, "My Garden." I was so proud of it. Since the science fair was in early May, my garden really wasn't much more than a big brown space. But it was a beautiful brown space. There were six pictures taped to the board of my garden from different angles, a picture of some tomato transplants, and a couple of trellises. Above each picture, my mom helped me make little bags from plastic wrap that I filled with tomato seeds, cucumber seeds, and other seeds. I was showing off what I loved and planted in "my own" garden. When the evening of the fair came, I was excited to go see my project, but not many other people were. I noticed most people walked by it. Some of my classmates asked me why I took pictures of dirt. Back then, I couldn't articulate what I can today. I couldn't articulate that seeds are magical. In one hand we can hold enough seeds to grow a garden and feed a family. My classmates just saw dirt. I saw magic and what my garden was going to

become. I still feel it every year when I walk into my early spring garden. I think you understand what I'm saying. Don't doubt your decision and desire to build your modern homestead. Don't feel you have to explain yourself to people who don't see what you see. Go out, enjoy your journey, build it, and let them see for themselves what you create.

A Word of Composting Caution

Fresh-cut grass clippings are a wonderful source of nitrogen-rich green material for your compost pile, but you have to proceed with caution. Never use clippings from grass that has had chemicals applied to it to control weeds. Unfortunately, all garden plants can be damaged by chemical residue. I learned the hard way when I collected freshly bagged grass clippings from my neighbors. I used them to cover my tomato garden, and within about a week, all the new plant growth was curled and deformed. While it didn't kill my tomato plants, it greatly damaged them. Grass clippings should be free of any chemical applications for several months before adding them to your compost pile.

All organic matter will decay and break down over time into usable compost, with smaller pieces breaking down more quickly. A log may take a decade, while a pile of finely shredded wood may take just a few months to fully compost. The reason for this is simple: microbes break down organic matter more quickly when they have more surface area on which to feed. Why is this important? The smaller the pieces, the more quickly you will get completed compost. Grass clippings are a great example of the ideal size compost materials should be. There are two basic ways you can compost. Let's talk about each.

MATERIALS FOR THE COMPOST BIN

Greens—nitrogen-rich materials	Browns—carbon-rich materials
Food scraps (fruits and vegetables are best)	Dry leaves
Green grass clippings	Wood chips (finely shredded is best)
Green leaves from tree trimming	Straw
Weeds	Sawdust
Coffee grounds (even though they're brown)	Dried cornstalks
Tea leaves and bags	Newspaper (cut into pieces)
Fresh animal manures	Cardboard (cut into pieces)
	Dried brown grass clippings
Material cut or shredded into small pieces will decompose more quickly.	

HOT COMPOSTING

Hot composting is the quickest way to break down organic matter into compost. This method is all about layering different types of organic matter to maximize microbial activity. Heat is a byproduct of microbes breaking down organic matter. You can speed up the rate of composting by mixing the right ratios of green materials (nitrogen) and brown materials (carbon). This is where people often feel compelled to get the "exact" ratios on layering materials. It just doesn't work that way because we all have different materials available and these materials vary over the seasons. The focus should be on principles. The goal is to feed those microbes and accelerate the composting process, not to have an exact and perfect ratio of ingredients.

That being said, it *is* important to strive for a ratio of materials that generates heat and speeds up the decomposition process. The ratio of nitrogen to carbon is done by volume, not weight, when making the layers. When mixing or layering the different organic materials, you may see different ratios recommended as 2:1 or 1:2 or 1:1 (greens to brown), for example. If you're just getting started, I recommend a 1:1 ratio. That means you want equal amounts of brown and green materials in your pile. Don't pack the materials down when measuring. You can fill equally sized buckets, one being filled with greens and the other, browns.

To build a hot compost pile, add a layer of nitrogen-rich material and then a layer of carbon-rich material; alternate these layers until you have a 4- to 6-foot-wide (1.2 to 1.8 m) rounded pile that is about 5 feet (1.5 m) tall. Realistically, you won't have enough organic materials to initially build a pile with those dimensions, but you can make smaller piles that will heat up using this layering technique. I encourage you to experiment, learn, and adjust your ratios through experience. You won't get it right the first time—and don't need to. A pile that smells strongly of ammonia has too much green materials (nitrogen) in it. A pile that stays cool to the touch has too much brown materials (carbon) in it. Striking the right balance between greens and browns will start the pile on its way to heating to between 100°F and 160°F (38°C and 71°C), a temperature high enough to kill pathogens and weed seeds. Using hot composting, you

can get compost in six to eight weeks, but you also need to actively turn the pile a few times a month and keep the material moist. You can't fail when composting. A pile may not finish as quickly as you'd like, but it always finishes.

A hot compost pile will decrease in size over its first week as long as it stays heated. When it compacts, less oxygen is available throughout the materials. This is when you "fluff" the materials of a smaller pile with a pitchfork to aerate them. Aeration brings oxygen back into the mix, and it will help restart the active hot composting process. If the pile cools, add greens to heat it up again. You can also moisten the pile, if needed, but do not soak it. Moisture is needed to maintain the process.

If you want to aerate and accelerate the process of a larger pile, build a new pile next to it. Remove one-third of the left side and one-third of the right side of the original pile, and make that the center base of the new pile you're mounding. Take the remaining top half of the old pile and put it on top of the new pile. What's left is the core of the old pile. It may be viable compost or close to it. You can use some of it if you wish or move it to the top of the new pile. Moisten the pile, but don't soak it, and place the tarp back on the top of the pile (if you were using a tarp). Tarps help maintain moisture in the pile and prevent it from getting overly soaked by heavy rains. This process has variations, and you'll learn how to maintain the heat of the pile with practice.

COLD COMPOSTING

If you don't want to worry about adding the right layers of organic matter and regularly turning your pile, cold composting is a great way to get started. It's Nature's way. Nothing fancy to see or do. Just start by making piles of organic matter. Cold composting is something that happens over a long period. Over a year, you'll add to the top of the compost pile. It can be grass clippings, garden waste, vegetable scraps, leaves, hay, shredded paper, pieces of cardboard, or any organic matter. But don't add meat scraps or fat drippings; they tend to attract animals.

Once the pile reaches 4 to 5 feet (1.2 to 1.5 m) in height, wait for it to begin composting and breaking down. This will decrease its size as the materials decompose.

More materials can be added when the pile shrinks, or you can start a second pile. Worms will move into cold compost piles and digest the organic matter. What they leave behind is Nature's gold—worm castings! You don't get worm castings in hot compost piles because worms don't like hanging out in high temperatures. They might venture in later, after the compost is "fully cooked," but you don't get as many castings in hot compost as you do with the slower cold composting method. I have both cold and hot compost stations on my homestead.

PILES, BINS, CAGES, AND OTHER COMPOST-MAKING PLACES

A compost pile can be started in a structure such as a metal cage or a wooden frame built out of pallets. You can also opt for commercial bins. The designs for DIY bins are seemingly endless, but they should include openings for air to flow through the sides. One side should be open or have the ability to open so you can access the pile. The target dimension of a constructed bin is about 4 to 5 feet (1.2 to 1.5 m) square that can hold 4 to 5 feet (1.2 to 1.5 m) of materials.

Compost tumblers are another option. Different types of tumblers range in size from 10 gallons (38 L) up to 55 gallons (208 L). They can be used either for cold or hot composting. They are typically shaped like a barrel with a lid on it. The lid opens and closes with a lock or it's screwed into place. Compost tumblers cut down on odors. The compost tumbler is designed to spin so the materials can be rotated every few days to aerate them. This is a great way to get started learning about compost. If you want to use them for hot composting, then the ratio of greens to browns comes back into play. Many people just put their kitchen scraps in them and give them a spin. Over time, the materials break down into a very rich compost. A word of caution: larger tumblers can become difficult to turn as you fill them.

Harvesting a Compost Pile

Late fall or early spring is the easiest time to harvest compost. If you have a cold pile, remove the top two-thirds of the heap, placing it on tarp. Remove material until you get down that sweet-smelling, broken down, worm casting-filled, deep brown, organic compost. Take what's on the bottom and spread it across your garden beds. Return the materials from the top back to the bin or pile and continue to add new materials on top of it.

An oft-neglected aspect of composting worth reviewing is moisture. You always want the piles to remain moist, but not soaking wet. A tarp can be used to partially cover the pile to direct rain away from its center. Rain will still fall onto the outer edges of the pile, keeping it moist. Microbes need continued water to flourish. A tarp also keeps moisture in the pile during the hot periods of summer. By just getting started, you begin to create your endless supply of garden compost.

5
BUILDING EARTH AND RAISED BEDS

I **T IS IMPORTANT NOT TO ALLOW** that overwhelming feeling you may have to learn "everything" to develop into a barrier that prevents you from starting. Remember, plants have been growing for millions of years. They need sun, water, warmth, soil, and fertilizer. All you need to do is foster these five things in your new homestead garden beds and you'll be successful. Digging and planting is how you'll learn and develop your skills. Start outdoors directly in the earth; over time, perhaps you'll think about using greenhouses and other structures. But for now, there's plenty to grow in earth beds to keep you busy for years.

Basic Garden Bed Designs

I recommend two types of garden beds for new homestead gardeners. The first are mounded earth beds and the second are framed raised beds. I like growing in framed raised beds because I like their look and symmetry. But I also like the way an earth mound looks in a planting area. So I have both earth beds and framed raised beds in my fenced-in garden.

MOUNDED EARTH BEDS

Mounded beds have been used for centuries. The easiest way to build one is to first remove the top 1 inch (2.5 cm) of existing vegetation, whether it's sod or weeds, and compost it. You can also turn it under. Much of that top growth will die and decompose, but you'll need to weed your new bed a few times to remove any stubborn growth. I recommend making earth beds 2 to 4 feet (60 to 120 cm) wide with a length of 12 feet (3.7 m) or more.

Bed Width

They are many ways to frame, dig, and prepare both types of beds, but I recommend this main principle for any design you choose: Make the beds 2 to 4 feet (60 to 120 cm) wide. Your arms are about 2 feet (60 cm) long, meaning you can tend to the entire planting area just by walking around the bed to reach in from all sides. You'll never have to step into any growing areas. Walking across planting areas causes the soil to compact, and it can inhibit plant growth.

To Soil Test or Not to Soil Test

If the area where you're placing your garden beds has been supporting weeds and grass, you probably don't need a soil test right now. Regularly using compost and organic fertilizers will support your garden soil and help it stay healthy and balanced. If you're building your homestead garden in an area that's bare of weeds, grass, or any kind of significant green growth, that's a good sign to test your soil to see what's going on. Contaminants or nutritional issues could be the reason nothing grows there. I also recommend getting a soil test if a once-thriving garden stops thriving. In those cases, a soil test will let you know what you need to adjust to improve the soil. Otherwise, you are good to dig in and plant!

After any existing vegetation is removed, loosen the soil in the area to a depth of 10 to 12 inches (25.5 to 30 cm). Since you won't be walking on the beds, you won't need to turn the soil ever again. If you'd like, you can put a layer of cardboard down and build your mound on top. The cardboard helps suppress weeds that may pop up from beneath.

Once the soil's turned and loosened, the next step is to mound up the planting area by taking soil from the bed edges and piling it into the middle. Eventually, you'll get a nice trench around the bed with an elevated planting area in the middle. One of the benefits of mounding is the creation of the surrounding trench, because you can fill the trench with water, like a moat, and water the whole area that way. The mounded area, like raised beds that we'll discuss next, also helps improve drainage if your area has issues with standing water. The mound lifts the plants above the ground level where water can sit.

FRAMED AND RAISED BEDS

Technically, anything framed is a raised bed, but I make a distinction based on the height of the frame. Anything up to 6 inches (15 cm) is a "framed planting area" because you're primarily using the earth as the main planting medium. Anything taller than 6 inches (15 cm) is a "raised bed" since you'll be filling it with a planting mix. Some raised beds can be 2 feet (60 cm) tall. Depending on how tall the sides are, the framed area can really hold a lot of new soil and amendments. Raised beds are often used over rocky, sandy, or otherwise problematic soil. Vegetables establish nicely in the newly filled beds and their root systems also will still grow into the earth to access nutrients there.

Like earth beds, framed beds should also have a width of 2 to 4 feet (60 to 120 cm). This allows you tend to plants from all sides without walking in the planting area.

I like raised beds as the entire space can be planted. There aren't any trenches taking up space, and you can plant right to the edges of the bed. Framing beds allows you to put amendments and resources only in the space you're planting, saving money and time. Taller framed beds also address any drainage issues you might encounter in your homestead garden. Another benefit is that they tend to warm more quickly than flat earth beds or even mounded earth beds. Because they're raised, sun and rain quickly warm the soil. That means you can plant sooner, and seeds germinate more quickly.

The easiest way to build raised beds is using 3- to 4-inch (7.5 to 10 cm) decking screws and wooden boards. Pre-drill your screw holes so the screws don't split the wood. Secure the corners of the boards with a minimum of two screws. I suggest using one screw for every 2 to 3 inches (5 to 7.5 cm) of board height. Screws are preferred over nails because a warping board won't pull out a screw. You can even forego having to measure your boards for cutting, as most lumberyards will do it for you. You can get two 8-foot-long (2.4 m) boards, in whatever height you choose, and ask them to cut them in half. These will assemble to a nice 4- by 4-foot (1.2 by 1.2 m) square. You can get three 8-foot-long (2.4 m) boards and ask the lumberyard staff to cut one in half. The pieces will assemble into a perfect starting raised bed, measuring 4 by 8 feet (1.2 by 2.4 m). You can also frame your beds with brick, stone, or cinderblocks. I have even seen them cast in concrete. You can buy metal framed beds that have no bottom and are one piece; you just drop them where you want them. I have repurposed several fire rings, typically used for burning wood, as raised beds.

Filling Raised Beds

It can be expensive to fill raised beds. There are many ways this can be done and buying bagged products is the most expensive. It's worth calling local landscape companies and ordering garden soil to be delivered when filling many beds. They typically have a garden soil plus compost mix for delivery. Otherwise you can make your own using this basic formula: one-half peat moss (or substitute coco coir) and one-half garden soil mixed equally as your 50/50 base. This very similar to the container mix I make in chapter 6. The garden soil can be anything from your property, some of it can be dug from the bottom of your raised bed area, or it can be purchased in bags typically labeled "garden soil." Once you have the 50/50 mix, you can add compost and other amendments to it as you fill the new beds. A general rule of thumb, once the beds are filled, is to apply 1 to 2 inches (2.5 to 5 cm) of compost across the bed and work it in to a depth of 6 to 12 inches (15 to 30 cm).

Sunken Containers

I can't say I invented this principle, but I did resurrect the idea in my gardens as a way to conserve water, resources, and have a long and narrow, but very productive, planting row. Plus, I really like the way it looks, and it's extremely functional. You can repurpose 5- to 10-gallon (19 to 38 L) nursery pots into sunken containers by cutting away 50 to 75 percent of their bottoms. Arrange them to form a long row of twenty to thirty containers, each sunk halfway into the ground with their sides barely touching. Fill the containers with basic container mix (I'll share my favorite recipes in chapter 6).

Plant the containers as you wish; I like growing peppers, kale, and determinate tomatoes in them. You can also use larger containers, such as 20 gallons (76 L), as stand-alone sunken containers placed throughout your homestead garden. I like growing indeterminate tomatoes, squash, zucchini, cucumbers, and okra in these larger containers. During the cool season, I plant them with peas and loose-leaf lettuce. They're a quick and easy way to get growing quickly. They aren't true containers because the plants' root systems quickly go down into the earth, and watering is not as much of a concern as it is in container gardening.

Soil Amendments

PEAT MOSS AND COCO COIR

Peat moss is a good all-around amendment to loosen soil for aeration, for drainage, and to retain moisture. Finely milled coco coir can also be used, or you can use a combination of both as I have mentioned. These amendments don't have any real nutritional value, but they're good for setting up new beds.

ORGANIC FERTILIZERS

Any balanced organic fertilizer is a good addition to new beds. The fertilizer's label instructions will typically tell you how much apply over a certain amount of square footage. If you're preparing a bed space that's 4 by 8 feet (1.2 by 2.4 m), you have 32 square feet (3 m²) to cover. To be honest, I don't measure. I simply scatter about four big handfuls evenly across a bed of that size. If you feel your hands are small, go with six handfuls. Once the different fertilizers are scattered, mix them in well to root depth.

COMPOST AND MANURES

Compost and manures are wonderful amendments. You just want to make sure that any manures you're using to set up new beds have been fully composted. If you apply manure that's fresh (and not broken down), it will finish its composting process in your garden bed and possibly compete with plants for nitrogen. Apply a total of 2 inches (5 cm) of compost, manure, or a mixture of both across the planting bed, and mix in to a depth of 12 inches (30 cm).

These are the main amendments I recommend when setting up new beds. You can also put a couple handfuls of lime across the bed if you're concerned the acidity of the peat moss will make your soil more acidic. Lime is alkaline and will raise pH levels. Lime is also a good source of calcium. If you want to add calcium to your beds without potentially raising soil pH, you can use a couple handfuls of gypsum. Worm castings can certainly be added, but I find they're best used in the actual planting area when you sow seeds or drop transplants into the beds.

If you don't have an area large enough to set up earth or raised beds, consider starting your homestead garden in containers. Next, I'll take a deep dive into growing edibles in pots. They're an excellent addition to your garden, even if you're also growing in beds.

6

HOMESTEAD CONTAINER GARDENING

THERE ARE TWO BASIC WAYS TO GROW PLANTS in your homestead gardens: in the ground or in containers. The essential difference is that in-ground beds have a complete thriving community of microbes, worms, and other soil organisms. Everything Nature created is hopefully alive and well in your soil. Container gardening does not have this community of life in the soil mixes we use. But that's okay. We don't need to replicate ground soil in our container mixes; instead, we need to make different choices for plant health.

Container gardening is all about providing the right-sized container for each plant variety, and providing soil that is loose, holds water, and has nutrients to support growth. It's really an artificial growing environment, even when it's 100 percent organic. First, we need to ensure that each plant has the right-sized growing area to meet its needs when it's fully mature. A tiny transplant looks very cute in a tiny pot, but a mature plant looks very sickly in a tiny pot. Even wonderfully loose soil can't correct problems that occur when a plant's root system is pot-bound and can't thrive. The wrong container size, a soil mix that doesn't hold water, and infrequent watering and fertilizing are the reasons we fail at container gardening.

Container Size and Drainage Holes

You can grow in pots that are deep and narrow, or you can grow in pots that are wide and shallow. Each plant grows best in a different type of container. I can't give you an exact pot size for plants because there's a wide range of pot sizes that will work, depending on what you want to grow. A good rule of thumb is that a pot can be too small, but it can never be too large. For instance, indeterminate tomatoes can be grown in pots ranging from 5 to 20 gallons (19 to 76 L) I have grown them in 5-, 10-, 15-, and 20-gallon (19, 38, 57, and 76 L) containers. The main difference is watering. When the plants get to be 4 to 5 feet (1.2 to 1.5 m) high, and it's mid- to late summer, a plant's watering needs can double or even triple for smaller pot sizes. In the middle of July, I was watering tomato plants in a 5-gallon (19 L) container two to three times a day. In a 15- or 20-gallon (57 or 76 L) container, I was able to water them once a day without concern.

Now, growing a tomato plant in a 1-gallon (3.8 L) container will never work, even if you can water a dozen times a day. You still need a minimum size for root growth. A plant needs to feel it has enough room to fully mature. If you're growing tomatoes in a milder summer climate, you can probably grow them in a 5- to 10-gallon (19 to 38 L) container. If you're growing them in areas with high heat summers, you'll need a 10- to 20-gallon (38 to 76 L) container based on the tomato variety. If you have doubts, purchase a container larger than you might think you need.

The other key to good container choice is drainage holes. It's so important to regularly water your plants, but at the same time, you can't let a plant's root system sit in water. Their roots will rot. All containers should have a minimum of three drainage holes, in case one gets blocked, about the size of a pencil eraser or a little larger.

Filling Your Containers

Another major factor in the success of your homestead container plantings is what you fill the pot with.

BAGGED MIXES, COMPOSTS, AND MANURES

The most expensive way to fill your plant containers is with bagged potting soil products. They're convenient but much more costly than making a container mix yourself, which are really pretty simple to make. Just about all commercial bagged products are made with varying amounts of peat moss. It holds water and keeps the soil medium loose, two must-have qualities for any soil used in container gardening. If you like the convenience of buying container soil and don't mind the expense, it's important to know what you're buying because all mixes are not the same. Going into a nursery can be confusing—there are so many soil products. You will typically see bagged products labeled as "topsoil," "premium topsoil," "garden soil," and "potting mix." Potting mixes have the most peat moss in them, and they are made for filling container pots. I recommend buying potting mixes.

You'll also find different types of bagged manures and compost vary greatly in quality. It's true that manures and compost can be used, in part, when filling your containers.

However, manures or compost you buy must be fully composted and not still be in the process of actively breaking down. As mentioned earlier, if you mix manures or compost with your potting mix and they're not fully composted, they will compete with your plants for nitrogen. Compost and manures that aren't "done" need nitrogen to finishing composting. The only way to really know the quality of bagged manures and composts is to talk with someone who's familiar with them. Another option is to try them, and you'll have your answer based on whether your plants flourish or struggle. When you find good products, stick with them.

Focusing on Container Success

I'm going to spend more time talking about pot sizes, soil mixes, and fertilizing than about what you can grow in your pots. There's a good reason for this. The bottom line is that you can grow nearly anything in a pot if you match the container to the needs of the plants. Learning and experimenting is part of the beauty of having your own homestead but I hope to save you a lessoned learned. I cannot stress these points enough: success is found in having a great potting/container mix, keeping plants watered and fertilized, and selecting the right-sized pot.

Making Your Own Container Mixes

It would be easy for me to tell you to make all your potting mixes with one-third to one-half of the mix being well-aged compost. However, I know that it's not that easy to have piles of compost just sitting around, waiting to be used, and buying compost can be expensive. I also know if I provide a recipe, many of you will feel that it has to be followed. That's not true. Rather than focus on using a specific recipe, focus on one basic principle: moisture retention. Potting mixes need to hold water. Peat moss, coco coir, and compost, or various combinations of all three, serve that purpose. Compost has the added benefit of supplying plants with the nutrients they need. Peat moss and coco coir have very little nutritional value for plants, but they're outstanding at holding water. Your container plants will be damaged if your container mix fully dries out, even once.

You can make your own outstanding moisture-retaining potting mixes by using the chart on page 102 as a guide.

CONTAINER MIX RECIPES AND RATIOS

	Peat Moss	Coco Coir	Compost	Earth
Potting Mix 1	50%	0	0	50%
Potting Mix 2	0	50%	0	50%
Potting Mix 3	25%	25%	0	50%
Potting Mix 4	50%	0	25%	25%
Potting Mix 5	0	50%	25%	25%
Potting Mix 6	0	0	50%	50%
Potting Mix 7	0	0	75%	25%
Potting Mix 8	0	0	100%	0%

Finely milled peat moss comes in compressed bags, and it goes a long way. Coco coir can be found in compressed bricks or loose in bags (make sure you get milled coco coir and not the large chunks that are often used in landscaping). Earth is the soil from your yard or a local source if needed. You're going to mix them using equal parts. "Equal parts" just means that you'll measure them using the same-sized container. For instance, that old bucket you have laying around is perfect for measuring. The filled bucket is one part. Using Potting Mix 1 recipe as an example, it would be 1 bucket of peat moss and 1 bucket of earth, which totals 100 percent of a 50/50 mix. If you need ten times that amount, use 10 buckets of peat moss and 10 buckets of earth. I recommend blending your mixes in a large wheelbarrow or on a tarp. Fertilizer can be added to the mix later. Potting Mix 5 is made with 2 buckets of coco coir, 1 bucket of compost, and 1 bucket of earth. The ratio is 2:1:1 or 50%:25%:25%. The percentages should always equal 100 percent.

I prefer Potting Mixes 1 to 5 as they contain peat moss and/or coco coir. They really create a loose, aerated soil structure while retaining moisture. Peat moss and coco coir maintain their structure and that keeps the container mix in great shape for several years. Compost needs to be replaced yearly as it simply gets used up. In my opinion, the best mix is 50 percent peat moss or coco coir, 25 percent compost, and 25 percent soil.

Now that we made our mix, let's talk about watering and fertilizing your containers properly.

Watering Practices and Principles

A common question I get is, when do I water my plants? The real answer, of course, is, when they need it. It's very hard to overwater a container plant in a pot that has drainage holes. When in doubt, water your container plants.

The basic watering principle is to water container plants every three to four days when plants are small and the temperatures are cooler. You'll need to increase that frequency to every two to three days as your plants get larger and the temperature begins to rise. When plants are mature and summer heat has set in, you'll have to watch them carefully. They'll easily need to be watered every other day, and in some cases, once or even *twice* a day. Container mixes dry from the top down, so the bottoms of your containers will stay wet the longest. Check containers by digging down about 1 inch (2.5 cm) and looking for dark, moist soil. If it appears light and dry, it's time to water. I find it's easier to follow a routine and set a schedule. Your plants will also tell you when soil moisture is low. The leaves will get limp and droop. You don't really want that to happen, as it does stress the plant, but if you notice it, water them immediately.

Mulching Containers

Mulching is a great way to help conserve water. A lot of evaporation comes off the surface of container mixes as the hot sun continually shines on them. As the mix dries, water wicks up from the bottom and redistributes itself to the top of the soil surface. I recommend spreading 1 to 2 inches (2.5 to 5 cm) of mulch on the top of your containers. Mulch helps regulate soil temperature, slows evaporation, and conserves moisture. I prefer using a finely shredded hardwood mulch for the job.

My garden gets a lot of rain so watering my containers really isn't an issue until mid-June. I water my very large container garden (that's located in my main garden) by hand early in the season. I use this time to inspect the plants and see how the garden is progressing. I switch to a sprinkler for watering my main garden and container garden once hot summer days arrive. I have a watering schedule set. I also have container plants scattered across my property and continue to water them by hand through the entire season. Another solution for watering containers is to install an automatic drip irrigation system. It is extremely useful for areas that have really hot summers, especially when your container garden is centralized.

Fabric Pots and Saucers

If you're growing in areas with very hot summers, a combination of fabric pots and saucers or trays can make a difference in your overall success. Fabric pots easily absorb water. You can buy plastic saucers with 1- or 2-inch (2.5 or 5 cm) sides at most stores. You can also use foil roasting pans or something similar. The saucers and trays are perfect for creating a water reserve. Thoroughly water plants growing in fabric pots as you normally would, fully saturating the container mix. Next, fill the saucer or tray with water. The sitting water will continue to water the plant for a day or two based on the plant size and temperatures. This is a great way to water plants if you have to go away over a weekend. This can also be done with solid containers, but the fabric pots work best.

Fertilizing Containers

I am guilty of playing mad scientist over the years and adding a little of this and dash of that to my container mixes under the guise of fertilizing. The truth is, most of the time, it isn't needed. Plants just need the basics, as I described in chapter 4. For containers, use a combination of a granular slow-release organic fertilizer and a water-soluble organic fertilizer. Here's how.

You Don't Have to Buy It—Nature Has It

Mycorrhizae are fungal organisms that form a symbiotic relationship with plants by colonizing their root system. They help a plant's roots acquire nutrients in exchange for some sugars exuded by the roots. Probiotics is the term often used to refer to soil microbiology. These are basically fungi, bacteria, and other organisms present in your native soil. Manufacturers of bagged soil mixes are now adding these elements to their products. I want to discuss this because basic container mixes lack the diverse soil microbiology found in your earth beds. At first, buying products such as these seem to make sense. However, soil microbiology quickly multiplies when it has food such as the basic ingredients that make up organic fertilizers. There's really no need to buy fancy "boosted" potting soils. Instead, use organic fertilizers regularly in your containers, throw in a few handfuls of soil from your garden beds or some compost, and you've pretty much seeded your container mix with all of the microbiology mentioned here. They'll begin to multiply. Keep gardening simple; do what Nature intends.

GRANULAR SLOW-RELEASE ORGANIC FERTILIZERS

For container plantings, I recommend trying to find a granular fertilizer that has an N-P-K ratio around 5-5-5. Finding a balanced granular fertilizer like this can be challenging. That's okay. A 6-3-4, a 4-6-2, or a 7-4-4 will work perfectly fine. I set my container mixes up with granular fertilizer when I fill the containers at the start of the season or when I dump out and refresh older mixes before planting. I fill the container halfway, add 2 to 3 tablespoons (30 to 45 ml) of fertilizer per square foot of planting space, and mix well. I fill the second half of the container and follow the same process. I add a total of 4 to 6 tablespoons (60 to 90 ml) of organic fertilizer per square foot of planting space.

ORGANIC WATER-SOLUBLE FERTILIZERS

Container plants also need to be fed with a water-soluble organic fertilizer once or twice a month. Regular feedings are key to successful container gardening. The N-P-K ratio of various organic water-soluble fertilizers will vary, but the goal is to make sure they're all

represented. I prefer using fish emulsion, which is a 5-1-1. There's no exact fertilizing routine but try to follow a logical pattern. Use less water-soluble fertilizer when the plants are small and more when they're larger. The frequency of fertilizing is every three to four weeks when the plants are small and every two to three weeks when the plants are large. If the plants are producing heavily, you can use a water-soluble fertilizer every ten to fourteen days. If you're going to use the chemical type fertilizers, they tend to have very high nitrogen ratios. Use them at half the recommended mixing.

A Sheet of Paper Is Close Enough to a Square Foot

A square foot is a bit more than a standard sheet of office paper. To figure out how many tablespoons (ml) of fertilizer to use, count the number of pieces of paper it takes to cover the surface area of your container. You can cut the sheet of paper in half lengthwise to measure narrow flower boxes. Shallow pots should be filled to the top, not halfway, before adding the appropriate measure of granular fertilizer.

When they're mature, container plants quickly use fertilizers. For an added boost, topdress your container with compost or worm castings monthly. If you don't have these amendments, use some organic granular fertilizer. Topdressing means scattering them across the top of the soil's surface. To keep it simple, add about 1 handful per square foot (0.09 m²) of container surface. Try to stay a couple inches (cm) away from the main stem when scattering it.

CONTAINER GARDENING WITH LARGER CROPS

Crop	Minimum Soil Volume (Requires Increased Watering)	Recommended Soil Volume	Tips
Tomato, Determinate	5 gallons (19 L)	10 gallons (38 L)	Increase water-soluble fertilizer to every 10–14 days when fruit sets.
Tomato, Indeterminate	10 gallons (38 L)	20 gallons (76 L)	Increase water-soluble fertilizer to every 10–14 days when fruit sets.
Pepper	5 gallons (19 L)	10 gallons (38 L)	Plant 2 per pot in 5- to 10-gallon (19- to 38 L) pots.
Eggplant	5 gallons (19 L)	10 gallons (38 L)	Use bamboo stakes to support branches.
Bush Squash	10 gallons (38 L)	20 gallons (76 L)	Harvest often and don't let the squash get oversized.
Bush Zucchini	10 gallons (38 L)	20 gallons (76 L)	Harvest often and don't the fruit get oversized.
Bush Cucumber	10 gallons (38 L)	20 gallons (76 L)	Plant 2 in a container for pollination. Trellis them up a tomato cage.
Vining Squash	15 gallons (57 L)	25 gallons (94 L)	Feed frequently with a water-soluble fertilizer.
Vining Zucchini	15 gallons (57 L)	25 gallons (94 L)	Feed frequently with a water-soluble fertilizer.
Vining Cucumber	15 gallons (57 L)	25 gallons (94 L)	Plant 2 in a container and trellis them.
Bean (Pole Type)	10 gallons (38 L)	15 gallons (57 L)	Plant 3–5 beans per container and harvest regularly.

There are many plants other than listed in this chart that grow well containers. The chart in chapter 3 on pages 74 to 75 shows general spacing and container-size requirements for many other vegetable crops.

The first sign that plants use to tell they need to be fertilized more often is yellowing of the lower leaves. Nitrogen is mobile within a plant, and the plant moves it to new growth, sacrificing the older leaves. A water-soluble fertilizer is immediately available to plants, so you should notice leaf greening within several days after use. The plants will recover, and you should increase your frequency of water-soluble fertilizing.

It's possible to love your plants to excess and give them too much fertilizer. However, that's hard to do with organic fertilizers. You generally want to keep a low and steady supply of nutrients available to container plants over the growing season.

Growing in Shallow Containers

Shallow containers can't maintain the moisture needed for larger plants, but they can really add to your container garden. Any flower box or pot with a depth of 4 to 6 inches (10 to 15 cm) or more is perfect for loose leaf lettuces, radishes, spinach, and even onions. They make wonderful herb boxes and can house chives, oregano, basil, thyme, and other herbs that stay below 18 inches (45 cm) of growth extremely well. All of these plants can be grown in larger pots too.

Starting an Herb or Greens Container Garden

Growing herbs is a great way to start your adventure in homestead container gardening. Three great herbs are oregano, thyme, and chives. They are perennial in many areas, meaning they'll come back year after year. I recommend starting seeds 8 to 10 weeks early indoors or buying transplants for this project. This will allow you to harvest these herbs the same season you plant them. Plant them about 6 inches (15 cm) apart in a flower box with a minimum depth of 6 inches (15 cm). You can plant them outside early because they are hardy and can take a frost. They're best planted in a 5-gallon (19 L) container. Plant them equal distances apart based on the width of the pot. The herbs will get larger in a pot versus a flower box because the roots have more room to grow. However you decide to plant them, you'll get plenty of herbs.

Container Gardening Fruit Crops

Strawberry plants are a perfect pairing with shallow containers. You'll need ten to twelve plants for a good harvest. They love the sun and need to be kept well-watered and fed. Strawberries can overwinter in cold climates. I recommend growing them in a flower box that's about 6 inches (15 cm) deep. Strawberry plants should be planted much more closely in flower boxes than in the ground; a distance of 4 to 6 inches (10 to 15 cm) apart is ideal. Other great fruit crops for containers are blueberries, blackberries, raspberries, and figs. They can be grown in 5- or 10-gallon (19 or 38 L) containers, as minimum sizes, planting one plant per container. Blackberries and raspberries will send up new canes and multiply. It may take two seasons to get a good harvest from fruit crops. If you decide to grow blueberries, it's important to grow two varieties for the purpose of cross-pollination. I'll discuss growing fruit crops in more detail in a later chapter.

7

TENDING YOUR GARDENS

ONE HOPE WE HAVE AS GARDENERS, new and old, is for a book to tell us how to tend and care for our gardens so we don't have any problems. Books can provide a wonderful overview of instructions, practices, and principles to care for a garden, but each garden has a unique set of issues. These include temperature, length of growing season, amount of rain, types of disease, and types of insects and wildlife. The best thing you can do is keep a journal of when problems arrive, what the problems are, and how you addressed them. You can manage problems and learn how to reduce damage, but many of the same problems will come back again around the same time every year. This is why keeping a journal helps. That's how I build management plans for my gardens.

In this chapter, I discuss basic tending and care practices for a garden as a whole, not plant by plant. What we each grow and how we have to care for our plants and manage our gardens varies—you may need to water your garden several times a week, while I only need to water mine once weekly—but the practices and principles hold true. I'll present basic skills you can adapt to your homestead garden's character and uniqueness. The best place to start is on the bottom.

Maintaining Healthy Soil

The first step to tending to your garden plants is tending to the soil life. I've written a good bit on the importance of healthy soil, so my focus here will be on maintaining fertile soil for the long term, not just when building a new garden. To keep your garden's soil and soil life healthy, apply 1 to 2 inches (2.5 to 5 cm) of compost to your garden beds every fall. You can turn it under or leave it on the bed's surface. Apply the same amount in early spring before planting. In addition to fall and spring applications, topdress your garden beds and containers during the middle of the growing season with 1 inch (2.5 cm) or so of compost. The more, the merrier your soil life will be.

Remember, no organic fertilizer, chemical fertilizer, or bagged product can do what compost does for your garden in the long run. It creates strong healthy plants that are better able to fight off pests and disease. Sourcing resources from our homestead and making compost is the original and true meaning of organic gardening. "Organic" originally meant materials made by Nature and collected around our property or community. It was never meant to be a commercial stamp. Part of becoming self-sufficient is moving away from commercial dependence. Composting may not be something you can do right away, but it's something you should set as a goal.

Preventative Care

The next step in caring for your homestead garden is to prevent problems before they arrive, either by an application or by an action you take. Sprays and dusts are used to manage pests and disease, and you'll learn more about them in chapter 8. But you don't want to rely on spraying *after* you see a problem. Once a disease or pest appears on your plants, a lot of damage may already be done, and more will likely follow. When you know early blight strikes your garden every July and attacks your tomato plants, start using preventative sprays in mid-June. You won't know all the problems that come to your garden, of course, but with time and experience (and lots of notes in your journal!), you'll learn what to look for and anticipate. Preventative care should be part of your weekly, if not daily, practice of tending to your garden. Talk to fellow local gardeners and nursery employees to ask them what problems are typical in your region.

Using a Journal—A Top Tool in My Garden

A journal is one of the top gardening tools to have at your disposal. It's always easy to remember everything from a day on that day, but if you're like me, two days later and I can't remember what I had for dinner. Write down the pests, diseases, and problems that show up in your garden. Write down the names of plant varieties that did well, did poorly, or got diseases, and make notes on changes that you may want to make to your routine or garden. It only takes a few minutes to jot down some notes and, believe me, you'll be glad you have them to refer to. This is the basic guideline I use for my entries when I encounter problems.

Date:

Plant:

Disease or pest name:

Description of how the problem affects your garden:

Temperature and weather condition of the last several days or week:

Treatment and outcome:

Ideas:

A journal should also note your successes, thoughts, and feelings you have as you're planting, tending, and building your homestead. It's a wonderful experience to look back at when you made a decision, implemented a change, learned something, or picked your first vegetable. I have a paper journal, a photo journal, and a pretty good collection of videos.

Tending to Your Homestead Garden

After soil care and prevention planning, the three most common tending tasks are watering, feeding, and managing growth. Remember, you started this journey by placing your gardens in the right place, you learned to match crops to the right temperatures and soil conditions, and you understand fruits and vegetables need good soil, sun, warmth, water, and compost. But your homestead garden also needs you to maximize growth and yields. Tending our gardens will vary week to week as the season progresses and crops change, but the best place to start is with water.

WATERING YOUR HOMESTEAD GARDEN

Most garden plants have extensive surface roots and roots that go deep into the ground. The roots' purpose is to acquire food and water. Plants get stressed when soil moisture is inconsistent, and that can cause problems. Stress inhibits growth and reduces flowering, fruiting, and overall production. Your vegetables will still produce, but not at yields they could have if they had been well-tended and watered. Stress also make it easier for diseases and insects to get a foothold on your plants. Underwatering is a common mistake in gardening.

Measuring How Much Water Comes from Your Hose or Sprinkler

To figure out how much water your plants are getting from a hose or sprinkler, try this trick. Take a 5-gallon (19 L) bucket and mark lines inside from the bottom at 1 inch (2.5 cm) high and another at 2 inches (5 cm) high. The general shape of a 5-gallon (19 L) container is pretty close to a 1 by 1 square foot (0.3 by 0.3 m²) and represents the base of a garden plant. Fill the bucket with your hose and time how long it takes for the water level to get to 1 inch (2.5 cm) and 2 inches (5 cm). That will be how long you have to leave the hose on your plant to give it 1 to 2 inches (2.5 to 5 cm) of water. You can also place the bucket in the field of your sprinkler and see how long you need to leave the sprinkler running until the water level in the bucket meets those measures.

Now that you've figured out how to measure and consistently give your plants 1 to 2 inches (2.5 to 5 cm) of water, you can figure out a watering schedule. You'll likely find that giving mature plants 1 inch (2.5 cm) of water a week isn't nearly enough to maintain optimum moisture consistency for maximum harvest. One inch (2.5 cm) of water is enough for plants to survive, but not to flourish. Using mulch helps maintain consistent soil moisture (on the soil surface) and reduces the need for more water. I suggest spreading 1 to 2 inches (2.5 to 5 cm) of mulch across your garden beds and in your containers to decrease how often you need to water and to also keep plant's surface roots moist as well. Use shredded hardwood, grass clippings, and compost as mulches. Start your watering schedule, using the following guidelines, and adjust it to your garden's needs over time.

Watering on a schedule and using mulch helps maintain consistent moisture in the soil. This consistency is greatly appreciated by plants, and it is essential in maintaining strong healthy plant growth and production. As your garden becomes larger, managing water becomes more challenging. You may have to progress from hand-watering to using sprinklers or even installing automated drip systems or soaker hose systems. The latter are primarily used in areas with prolonged high temperatures or by those who have very large gardens. I like watering my garden by hand when I can, as I use that time to look for pests and diseases.

It's generally stated that plants need at least 1 inch (2.5 cm) of water a week and the water should soak at least 5 inches (13 cm) into the soil. I generally agree, but how can we measure that? Let's figure out how much 1 inch (2.5 cm) of water is in a garden. Every homestead should have a rain gauge. Just because it rained doesn't mean your garden got enough water. Check the gauge after a storm and make sure your garden got 1 inch (2.5 cm) or more of rain. If it did, you can skip watering for a few more days.

Maintaining consistent moisture in your gardens reduces plant stress and prevents things such as fruit cracking, blossom end rot in tomatoes, and other physiological problems associated with watering inconsistencies. The preceding watering schedule may not be exactly what your homestead garden needs, but it sets you up with a beginning schedule.

WATERING FREQUENCY

	Earth Beds	Containers	Seeds & Seedlings
Early Spring	1x weekly	1x–2x weekly	1x–2x weekly, keep soil surface moist
Mid-Late Spring	1x–2x weekly	2x–3x weekly	2x weekly, keep soil surface moist
Early Summer	2x–3x weekly	3x–4x weekly	3x–4x weekly, keep soil surface moist
Mid-Late Summer	3x–4x weekly	Every other day & sometimes daily	Check daily, keep soil surface moist
Fall	1x–2x weekly	2x weekly	2x–3x weekly, keep soil surface moist
Rain of 1 inch (2.5 cm) or more can count as a day of watering.			
Seedlings don't have established roots, so you want to keep the soil surface moist until they're well established.			

Granular Fertilizers and Topdressing

Earth beds and raised beds are more forgiving of watering and fertilizing than container gardens, but the principles are pretty much the same. We discussed using granular fertilizers to set up your containers and garden beds before planting. Once planted, granular fertilizers are used as a topdressing on the soil's surface. Frequency will vary based on plant maturity size and a gardener's personal preference, but the minimum is a one-time topdressing at midseason for larger plants such as squash, zucchini, tomatoes, peppers, cucumbers, Brussels sprouts, cabbages, eggplants, and others. Plants that don't need a topdressing include lettuces, spinach, radishes, carrots, and arugula and other leafy greens. When in doubt, err on the side of topdressing. A topdressing could be using 1 inch (2.5 cm) of compost across the surface of the bed or scattering a few handfuls of the granular organic across the bed.

Water-Soluble Fertilizers and Frequency

You'll recall that water-soluble fertilizers provide nutrients that are immediately available to plants. Water-soluble fertilizers, in general, are more important to container plants than to plants growing in earth or raised beds. Container plants quickly use all the nutrients in the container soil, especially when they get to a certain size. The key to using water-soluble fertilizers is consistency. Every two weeks works for a water-soluble feeding, either for containers or earth beds, if you want to keep things simple. You can adjust it to every fourteen to twenty-one days when plants are small, and to every ten to fourteen days when plants are larger and producing.

Remember, when you are able to use your own compost regularly, you'll need to rely on the other fertilizers less often.

Staking, Pruning, and Trellising

You don't have to stake and prune plants if you don't want to. Plants will sprawl across the ground and still produce. However, their life's goal is reproduction, and our goal is to get high yields of fruits and vegetables. Trellising or staking your plants allows them to grow vertically. This uses space you wouldn't otherwise be able to use in your garden. Growing plants vertically allows you to plant more plants in

Pruning Tomatoes Is an Art, Not a Science

You often hear that tomato "suckers" should be removed because they take energy from that plant. That is true, but they also give energy to that plant. A sucker is actually a complete production stem. A tomato plant starts its life as a single vine, and it grows leaves, a flower cluster, more leaves, and another flower cluster; that original vine continues to grow, repeating the pattern. Sometimes we prune to keep only the single stem or vine growing and producing. That is called single-stem pruning, and you're essentially tending to and keeping the original vine. From the joint area, where a leaf attaches to the stem, you'll see new growth, which is commonly called a tomato sucker. The photos show you how it will grow into a production stem and flower. If you let it grow, it will continue to produce leaves, a flower cluster, and so on.

You now have two stems producing flowers and fruit, and sometimes people prune their tomato plants to two stems, removing all others. That is called double-stem pruning. However, just about every joint where a leaf meets a stem will produce a sucker. This becomes exponential growth of new vines, and this is how indeterminate tomato plants become massive. My pruning style has changed over the years. I gradually prune out 12 to 18 inches (30 to 45 cm) of the bottom growth when the plant reaches 4 feet (1.2 m) tall. This allows airflow between the soil and upper leaves and creates a disease splash barrier that prevents soilborne fungal spores from reaching the plant via splashes from rain and watering. I remove suckers and leaves to keep gaps in the upper growth of the plant and to keep the plant about 3 to 4 feet (0.9 to 1.2 m) wide. My goal is airflow and leaf management to reduce the spread of leaf diseases. Pruning is just about controlling plant size, typically for space and disease management. I suggest you experiment with pruning and watch how the tomato plant grows. Over time, you'll develop your own pruning style.

your garden, which will increase your overall harvest. It also allows you to manage pests and disease more easily. Cucumber vines will spread across the ground and shade out other plants. Tomato plants are actually vining plants that sprawl everywhere and take over a space when left unchecked. Summer squash and zucchini plants produce massive leaves, and their thick, heavy leaf growth can be a haven for insects and a place for air circulation to stagnate, allowing fungal spores to land, settle, and infect plant leaves.

You can trellis any vining plant as long as you support the weight of its mature fruit. Cucumbers, acorn squash, spaghetti squash, butternut squash, cantaloupe, other small melons, small pumpkins, gourds, and even some vining varieties of zucchini make great vertical growers. If the fruit can hang to maturity without tearing the vine, then you can stake or trellis it. If needed, make slings for the fruit and support them by tying the sling to the trellis. Pole beans are natural climbers. Place an 8-foot (2.4 m) pole in the ground, plant three seeds around it, and you'll get

CROP SUPPORT AND CARE

Common Garden Plants	Trellis	Stake	Prune	Benefits
Cucumber	X		Damaged leaf removal and minor vine removal if needed	Space saving and easier management of pests and diseases
Melon	X		Damaged leaf removal and minor vine removal if needed	Space saving and easier management of pests and diseases
Cantaloupe	X		Damaged leaf removal and minor vine removal if needed	Space saving and easier management of pests and diseases
Squash	X		Damaged leaf removal and light healthy leaf removal to manage airflow	Space saving and easier management of pests and diseases
Bean	X	X	Removal of leaves that have pests or disease	They naturally want to climb
Tomato, Determinate		X	Removal of leaves that have damage or disease	Manage space and keep them upright
Tomato, Indeterminate		X	Removal of some suckers, healthy bottom leaves, diseased leaves and mid-section leaves for airflow	Manage space and massive growth
Pepper		X	Removal of leaves that have damage or disease	Support the plant, to keep stems from breaking
Eggplant		X	Removal of leaves that have damage or disease	Support the plant, to keep stems from breaking
Large Sunflower		X	Removal of leaves that have damage or disease	Keep the plant from falling over or stem from breaking
Peas	X		None	They have hollow stems. Support the plant and upward growth.

a great harvest of green beans several weeks later. Determinate tomatoes don't need to be pruned (see the sidebar), but sometimes they need a small stake or wire cage to support their growth and keep them upright. Indeterminate tomatoes need to be staked and pruned if you want to manage their massive size and sprawling habit. How much tomato pruning you want to do is completely up to you.

The difference between staking and trellising is minimal, but staking is usually a single post or cage while a trellis is a more extensive support system. A post or stake is used to tie plants to it to encourage vertical growth, and a cage is used to support growth and keep a plant upright without tying the plant to it. A trellis is more elaborate, usually one foot to several feet wide, and it allows plants to climb along the surface using the plants own tendrils or a gardener can weave plants through it.

I sometimes prune my plants to remove damaged (diseased or infested) leaves, which I typically throw away. Anytime I'm working in my garden, I inspect the undersides of leaves and remove leaves and lightly prune for airflow. Very often you'll find insect eggs under the leaves, and pests and disease is the subject of chapter 8.

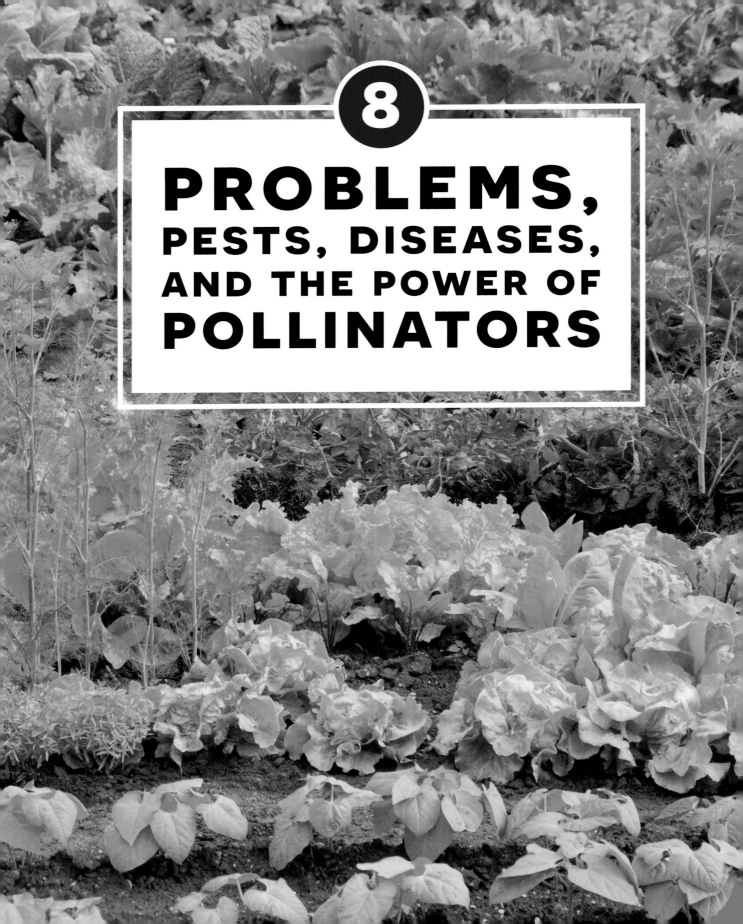

8

PROBLEMS,
PESTS, DISEASES,
AND THE POWER OF
POLLINATORS

EVERY GEOGRAPHICAL REGION HAS PESTS and diseases that are common to local gardens. Research and talk to local gardeners and nursery employees to find out what problems come to your region. Through research, conversation and observation, you're going to have to learn how to identify the problems, pests, and diseases that visit your garden. Most pests and diseases come at specific times when environmental conditions support their life cycle or routine. Your prevention and management practices will make it more difficult for them to establish in your garden, but every gardener faces issues from time to time. Don't become discouraged when you encounter problems. You'll learn how to manage them, and the garden will still produce.

The goal of addressing any problem in a garden is to manage losses. You won't be able to reduce pest and diseases 100 percent, and that shouldn't be your goal. No single product does it all, in a single application, and all gardens have unique problems, pests, and diseases. I was once asked how I prevent large lizards from eating my plants. I didn't have an answer to that question because I never even knew that was a common problem in other places.

It's important to understand that both organic and synthetic chemical products can be harmful to us, plants, bees and other good insects, and to animal life. Organic does not always equate to safe and harmless. It's good practice to read about any product you decide to use in your garden well before you use it. If you're going to use sprays, test spray new products. Test spraying means applying the product just to a few leaves of the plant and waiting 48 hours for potential damage. Test spraying is important because factors such as temperature and altitude can affect the way your plants react to different sprays. Test spray *each* plant variety as their leaves differ and may react differently to different sprays. I have

damaged plenty of leaves with baking soda spray. Two tablespoons (30 ml) mixed into 1 gallon (3.8 L) of water worked well on my plants with thicker leaves, such as kale, but damaged my plants with frail leaves. Always start with the lowest mix ratio first and work your way up—if needed—to the highest recommended dose. Using more doesn't necessarily mean it's more effective or faster-acting.

Products for dusting plants can be organic or chemical. Dusts that are contact killers will kill *all* insects, including pollinators. They should *not* be used on flowers or left on plants when pollinators are around. I recommend using them in the late evening and washing the leaves off the next morning when it's early (which is after/before pollinators are active). I try to keep these dust products off plants during the day. It's important to understand how these products work and when to use them. Again, I highly recommend a journal for recording your experiences.

Common Pests, Diseases, and Solutions

There are so many different products you can use in your homestead garden. I encourage you to learn about them all, as well as natural predators. Nature can help you deal with insect pests. I recently started attracting insect-eating birds by adding bird feeders and birdhouses to my garden, and I've seen them eat insects off my cabbages. You can buy nematodes and ladybugs and release them into your garden. You can use flowers to attract pollinators and predatory insects onto your homestead. I'll discuss some of these options at the end of this chapter, but let's start with products we apply.

You really only need four types of products in your homestead garden defense arsenal.

1. Something to manage chewing caterpillars
2. Something to manage beetles and other insects.
3. Something to manage fungal diseases.
4. Something to repel insects and mask plant scents.

Before we begin talking about these products, let's go back to something we discussed in chapter 4: healthy soil. Healthy soil makes for strong, healthy plants that are less attractive to insect pests and better able to fight off fungal attacks. The original theme of prevention starts with maintaining outstanding soil and healthy plants. Stressed and weak plants are more susceptible to insect attacks and diseases. However, healthy soil and plants aren't a 100 percent guarantee. Please don't be discouraged when insect and diseases show up; it's not your fault. It's just part of the journey. Each homestead garden will be subjected to different pests and diseases, but they all share common themes. It's important to walk through your garden several times a week and look for problems. The sooner you identify and address a problem, the better you can manage it and move on to a new garden project or task

CHEWING CATERPILLARS

Chewing caterpillars (often called worms) typically arrive as eggs, laid by moths and occasionally butterflies. Inspect the undersides of leaves and along leaf stems for eggs. The clusters often stand out, and once you see one, take action. I use Neem oil (see my recipe). Also look for small holes in leaves as that's how caterpillars start. Chewing worms typically hide from the hot sun. If you find worms, remove them by hand and also begin spraying. If you don't find worms, come back a couple days later and look to see if there are more holes. Take

beet army worm

hornworm

pictures if you need to for comparison. If so, begin looking diligently for the culprit. Common worms that attack my plants are tomato hornworms, cabbage worms, cabbage loopers, and armyworms. Neem oil spray will manage chewing worms and other chewing insects.

CHEWING BEETLES AND OTHER INSECTS

Beetles and other insects can fly in, crawl in, or sometime hatch in your gardens after overwintering in the soil or other areas on you homestead. They tend to be more active at night, but you can find them crawling on leaves during the day. My cucumber plants

Tools of the Trade for DIY Recipes

You'll need several 32-ounce (946 ml) spray bottles, two 1-gallon (3.8 L) pump sprayers, measuring spoons, and your journal. I write the recipe for each spray and the name on each 32-ounce (946 ml) spray bottle as well as in my journal. I use one pump sprayer for oils and one pump sprayer for non-oil sprays. These tools are essential. In addition to these, I save empty talcum or baby powder containers for dusts, such as diatomaceous earth. Soap is needed to disperse oils in water when the mix is shaken. Soaps can be a bit confusing and are worth discussing.

Soaps and detergents serve the same purpose in DIY pest treatments: They're used to help disperse oil-based products through water. Without soap, oil would float on the surface of the water, and you wouldn't be able to coat plant leaves evenly with whatever oil you are using. A pure soap, such as castile, is best as it doesn't have any other additives. You can use dish soaps, but they often contain detergents and other degreasers. I have used both and haven't noticed any issues, but you'll use detergent-based soaps at a much lower ratio in the gallon of water. If you are using anything that isn't a pure soap, start with 1 teaspoon (5 ml) in 1 gallon (3.8 L) of water, and mix well with the amount of oil the recipe recommends. Shake the sprayer and see if it remains dispersed in the water for at least 15 seconds before it floats back to the top of the water. Shake the spray bottle or pump sprayer every 15 seconds when spraying your plants. Add a little more soap if the oil isn't remaining dispersed for that long. Once you find the right combination of ingredients, write it down in your journal. Every time you change soap brands, you need to repeat this.

Always test spray leaves and wait 48 hours. If you see no damage, you can spray the entire plant. This is worth repeating because I have wiped out entire plants by not following this advice.

Neem Oil Spray and My DIY Recipes

Neem oil is often recommended for use against chewing insects, which seem to be the most affected by it. For Neem oil to be effective, it must be 100 percent cold-pressed Neem oil with no components removed. The chemical azadirachtin found in Neem oil is primarily responsible for its effectiveness. Unfortunately, many products have "Neem Oil" on the label, but what they actually are is a hydrophobic extract of Neem. It will say so under the ingredients somewhere on the label. It's misleading; what that means is the azadirachtin and some other components have been removed. It is only a pure oil at this point and is no more effective against chewing pests than olive oil.

NEEM OIL RECIPE

Prevention	Neem Oil Per Gallon of Water	Castile or Other Pure Soap	Soaps that Contain Detergents	Routine
Under 80 Degrees	1–2 tablespoons (15–30 ml)	1 tablespoon (15 ml)	1–2 teaspoons (5–10 ml)	Every 1–2 weeks
Over 80 Degrees	1 tablespoon (15 ml)	1 tablespoon (15 ml)	1–2 teaspoons (5–10 ml)	Every 1–2 weeks
Notes	Don't add other components to it.		Use caution with high detergent type soaps.	Moderate rain will increase frequency.
Infestation	Spray every 3–5 days for 3 cycles and return to preventative spraying.			
Spray Efficacy	The solution of Neem oil can last 5–7 days in a container that is stored out of sunlight and in a cool area.			

are always getting attacked by striped and spotted cucumber beetles. Rarely do I find their eggs or larvae in the soil, but I see the adults walking on leaves. They tend to arrive at the same time each year. Mexican bean beetles attack my bean plants regularly. The females lay clusters of thirty to forty eggs on the undersides of leaves, and the eggs, fuzzy yellow larvae, and adult beetles are easily spotted on the plants' leaves. My eggplants are devastated by flea beetles. I follow the same inspection process I do when I'm looking for chewing worms. Neem oil is less effective with these pests, but I use that in conjunction with other products.

You can use Spinosad in sprays and dusts. It is made by a specific soil bacterium and it's a natural product. Spinosad kills a wide array of insects. There is another natural substance called *Bacillus thuringiensis*, or Bt. It's also derived from a soil bacterium and is typically used as a spray. Using a combination of these three

cucumber beetle

flea beetle

Mexican bean beetle larvae

products is often very effective. Sprays are a good choice as they dry on leaves and only the chewing insects are affected. However, at times you may need a dust that's picked up by beetles that walk across it.

Any insect dust works but remember: They are indiscriminate killers. I highly recommend dusting late in the evening and washing it off early in the morning to reduce harm to beneficial insects. I recommend Spinosad in dust form first before moving to synthetic dusts. Dusts are extremely effective on beetles and crawling insects. Apply the dust to the plants' outer leaves and stems but stay away from their flowers. Beetles are very active at night and will find their way to the dust.

Another alternative you can try before using more potent applications is to dust the leaves with diatomaceous earth (DE). It's an extremely sharp natural microscopic silica. The DE dust gets into the joints of the beetles and other insects and "grinds" the protective coating off their shells and bodies. Very often, the insects dehydrate and die. Diatomaceous earth has to be replaced after a rain (because it washes away). DE is organic, and it comes in a large bag. I fill an empty talcum powder bottle with DE dust to make sprinkling the plant leaves easier.

powdery mildew

blight

FUNGAL LEAF DISEASES

I get powdery mildew on my cucumber, squash, and zucchini plants. I occasionally get leaf spot on my tomato plants, but they get early blight every year if I don't treat them. I know when these fungal diseases arrive, and preventative spraying allows me to manage these issues with minimal loss. It's best to start antifungal sprays before the problems arrive. If you notice powdery mildew, which actually looks like a powder on your leaves, or other fungal problems, remove the infected leaves and discard them. Do not compost; throw them away in the trash. Once problematic leaves are removed, begin your spraying routine.

leaf spot

My DIY Recipes for Baking Soda Spray and Wettable Sulfur Spray for Fungal Problems

When applied, these products change the pH value on plant leaves and make them inhospitable to fungal pathogens. Baking soda is alkaline and increases the pH level of leaf surfaces. Sulfur is acidic and decreases the pH level of leaf surfaces. These products can damage plant leaves, so you should test spray each plant variety. You can add some soap to help the baking soda or sulfur stick to the plant.

Spray every one to two weeks, but, more often if it rains moderately, and less often if you get a week or so of dry days. Spray the entire plant; cover the tops and bottoms of leaves and the stems. You cannot mix sulfur and baking soda and assume you'll get the double protection; they'll neutralize each other and provide no benefit whatsoever.

BAKING SODA AND WETTABLE SULFUR RECIPES

Prevention	Baking Soda or Wettable Sulfur Per Gallon of Water	Castile or Other Pure Soap	Other Soaps that Have Detergents	Routine
Under 80 Degrees	1–2 tablespoons (15–30 ml)	1 tablespoon (15 ml)	1–2 teaspoons (5–10 ml)	Every 1–2 weeks
Over 80 Degrees	1 tablespoon (15 ml)	1 tablespoon (15 ml)	1–2 teaspoons (5–10 ml)	Every 1–2 weeks
Notes		Soap is not needed but may help the material stick.	Use caution with high detergent type soaps.	Moderate rain will increase frequency.
Outbreak	Spray every 3–5 days for 3 cycles and return to preventative spraying			
Spray Efficacy	The solution of either of these two mixes can last 1 week or longer.			

Starting with Less in Your Mixes

Leaf damage can occur with any spray. One way to learn how your plants respond to sprays is to start with the fewest ingredients possible. Soap is needed to disperse oil sprays, but it's not needed in fungal sprays that use baking soda (though it can be added). Also start with the lowest mix dosage first. In the case of baking soda that's 1 tablespoon (15 ml). If the spray is effective, take notes and stick with that recipe mix. If it's not effective, raise the dosage. Leaves can tolerate sprays better when it's cooler. A spray that did no harm in spring can harm plants when the temperature gets over 80ºF (27ºC), and even more so when temperatures approach 100ºF (38ºC). You probably noticed plants wilt, even when watered, during periods of high temperatures. It's best not to spray wilting leaves and wait for a cool period. They're easily damaged by oils when in this state. If you can't wait, the alternative to spraying when it's hot is making sure you spray early in the morning or later in the evening, when temperatures are cooler.

Sprays to Repel Insects and Mask Plant Scents

squash bug nymph

Aphids are soft-bodied insects that appear on many different plants. They're easily spotted as dozens of them cluster on stems and leaves. They're usually green but can be yellow, orange, red, black, brown, or gray. Spider mites are very small and need to be viewed with a magnifying glass. They can be identified by their leaf damage, usually tiny yellow dots on leaf tops, and by bits of webbing on the undersides of leaves. The best way to control aphids and spider mites is to forcefully spray the undersides of any infected plant with water two to three times a week. These are both tiny and frail insects. Simple water spray can reduce their numbers. They don't crawl back onto the plants. I also use peppermint oil or rosemary oil sprays on spider mites and other very tiny insects (see the chart below).

aphids

PEPPERMINT OIL SPRAY

Peppermint oil is used to irritate and repel small insects, such as spider mites. Spider mites are very resistant to bug sprays and dusts and peppermint oil is often more effective. As mentioned, insect dusts are indiscriminate killers, and they often kill the predatory insects that feed on spider mites. Peppermint oil is an irritant and repellant to very small spider mites. The oil can also be used to mask plant scents, as many insects find host plants based on smell. When leaves or stems are damaged, pheromones from the plant are released, or they can be released naturally. Some insects find plants by following these scents. The strong scent of peppermint can mask plant odors and deter the arrival of unwanted pests.

PEPPERMINT OIL SPRAY RECIPE

Prevention	Peppermint Oil Per Gallon of Water	Routine for Scent Masking	Routine for Repelling Agitation
Under 80°F	1–2 teaspoons (5–10 ml)	1–2 times weekly	1 time weekly
Over 80°F	1 teaspoon (5 ml)	1–2 times weekly	1 time weekly
Spray Efficacy	In theory, this mix can last indefinitely but I recommend not letting it sit beyond 2 weeks.		

The spray routine for peppermint oil is the same for prevention or outbreaks. It's important to make sure you buy *essential peppermint oil* and not extract. I recommend the variety *Mentha piperita*, which is often noted on the oil label. I prefer the menthol level in this variety. My experience has shown it to be a greater irritant to spider mites.

SOAPY WATER SPRAY

I make my soapy water spray in a 1-gallon (3.8 L) sprayer. The recipe is pretty straight-forward: 1 tablespoon (15 ml) pure soap (such as Castile) in 1 gallon (3.8 L) of water. Soapy water spray is effective on soft-bodied insects such as aphids. The soap essentially dehydrates the insect. I direct spray the aphids.

Using Flowers to Attract Pollinators and Predatory Insects

All gardens need pollinators. Flowers such as marigolds, purple coneflowers, bee balm, borage, and sunflowers attract bees and other pollinators. They should be planted throughout your garden and around your property. Along with attracting pollinators to help improve my harvests, they also attract predatory insects that feed on the pest insects causing problems, thus reducing the number of potentially problematic insects. I have a butterfly garden, away from my main garden, that attracts all kinds of insects.

In a corner of my main garden, I have what I call a good bug "hotel." It has hiding and nesting areas for beneficial insects. Sitting on top of it is a container of flowers. Next to it, I have a five-tiered tower planted solely with flowers. I have daisies, yarrow, coreopsis, and different coneflowers planted in containers along the inner fence line of my main garden. I also have a wildflower garden planted along the edge of my woods.

Nature provides many alternatives for dealing with harmful insects. These alternatives work but often are overlooked. Broken clay pots serve as homes for toads and frogs that love eating slugs and snails. Bird feeders attract birds, which eat weed seeds and insects. Bird houses encourage birds to nest and the parent birds will feed garden pests to their growing young. A bird bath with a solar sprinkler on it provides water for birds, predatory wasps, and dragonflies, all of which enjoy eating insects, especially mosquitoes and caterpillars.

9

CREATING AN EDIBLE LANDSCAPE ON YOUR HOMESTEAD

WHEN I WAS THINKING ABOUT WHAT TO INCLUDE in this book, I was excited to think about writing about fruit and nut trees. I was going to cover the specifics of growing apples, peaches, pears, cherries, nectarines, tangerines, and plums, which are basically all the fruit trees I'm growing in my own homestead garden. But then I realized that *what* I'm growing is far less important than *why* I'm growing it. Instead, I'll discuss how I'm using berries, bushes, canes, vines, and fruit and nut trees to build an edible landscape on my homestead. I may not be growing what you want to grow, or I may be growing something that won't thrive or survive in your region, but the principle behind building an edible landscape is universal. Learning to be more self-sufficient and less reliant on commercial markets for food means growing everything you can, including fruits and nuts. The good news is that we can all add these food sources to our properties because they can be grown just about anywhere. Yes, you can grow fruit trees on your balcony in containers, or you can plant a full-blown orchard on a large homestead, or you can do something in between. Because whatever size your property is, you can add fruit and nuts to your homestead.

Let's start by taking a look at some of the best fruit crops for your modern homestead garden.

Fruit Crops

STRAWBERRIES

Strawberries are perennial, meaning they come back year after year. They are very hardy and can take freezing temperatures for prolonged periods. You can look up varieties in catalogs and online to see if they can survive winters in your area. They're available in early-, middle-, and late-ripening varieties, and there are even varieties that provide two harvests over the season. I recommend planting

at least two varieties that ripen at different times. Strawberries are versatile and can be planted in shallow flower boxes, larger containers, strawberry towers, raised beds, and in the ground. I plant mine along a fence where one might normally grow landscape plants. Strawberries make wonderful replacements for standard groundcover plants, and they can be planted just about anywhere that gets six or more hours of sunlight a day. They reproduce quickly and easily, and they'll provide many new plants to place throughout your homestead. Strawberries prefer to be planted in areas that drain well.

MULBERRIES

There are so many different varieties of mulberries that I'm sure several will suit your area. They are winter-hardy tree fruits and best transplanted in spring after the danger of frost has passed. Mulberries like full sun and do best is soil that drains well. Be careful, though. Mulberries come in dwarf varieties that grow several feet tall, and tree varieties that can pass 50 feet (15 m) tall! They grow quickly and can be used for their fruit and as shade. They're great additions to your edible landscape.

Mulberries can manage some shade, but fruit best when in full sun. Black mulberries are said to have the best-tasting fruit, but red mulberries can handle lower winter temperatures.

Basic Planting Guidelines for Fruiting Trees and Shrubs

Any fruiting bush or tree can be planted using this general method.

Step 1: Dig your hole to the same depth as the root mass of the plant or a little bit deeper. Many sources say to dig the hole twice as wide as the container, which is fine if you have a 12-inch (30 cm) container, but that's really big if you have an 18- or 24-inch (45 or 60 cm) container. Set the container down and mark 6 inches (15 cm) from the container's edge all the way around the container. That's how wide to dig your hole no matter the size of the container.

Step 2: Loosen the soil in the bottom of the hole 6 to 12 inches (15 to 30 cm) down and leave the soil in place. The planting hole is ready. You don't need to add a lot of fertilizer to the planting hole. A handful mixed well into the bottom of the hole is perfect.

Step 3: Place the plant into the hole, about even with the soil surface, and backfill with the soil that came out of the hole. Make sure you don't leave any large air pockets.

Step 4: Mulch is helpful to maintain moisture but not necessary. Cover the planting area with about 1 inch (2.5 cm) of mulch if you decide to use it.

Step 5: Water the plant in well. Watering is the key to success. Water your bush or tree a couple times a week for the first couple of months and at least once a week until the plant is well established.

Use Blueberries and Fruit Crops Everywhere

To create a truly edible landscape, think about using them where you might plant decorative plants, bushes, and groundcovers. I have a formal planting area for my blueberries, strawberries, and raspberries. I also use blueberries as decorative bushes along my white picket fence. Not only will I be able to get fruit from them, but once they establish, they'll also have beautiful foliage that changes colors in autumn. I try to put plants in the ground that will either bring food to my table, pollinators to the garden, or flowers to a vase.

GOJI BERRIES

Goji berries have become more popular in recent years. I have several in my yard. The goji berry, also known as the wolfberry, is a shrub that can have a 4-foot (1.2-m) spread and grow over 10 feet (3 m) tall. If they aren't pruned, they can grow into a tree. They are rich in vitamins, antioxidants, and minerals. I find their taste bland, but for others, they are the perfect addition to salads, sauces, and even pasta dishes, and they're a great way to get your vitamins and minerals.

Goji berries are very hardy and can take long, deep-freeze winters. They also make great container plants and should be planted in a 10-gallon (38 L) container or larger. They're easy to grow and can be grown from rooted 8-inch (20 cm) cuttings in smaller pots until they leaf out and are about 1 foot (30 cm) tall.

Goji berries should be planted 4 to 6 feet (1.2 to 1.8 m) apart and just left to grow their first year. They'll come back in force the second year and can be pruned to manage size. Many people grow them as one would grow grapes along a fence. They'll typically produce some fruits in the first year but tend to produce much more heavily in their second or third years. Berries begin to ripen in midsummer and continue until frost.

BLUEBERRIES

I recommend growing blueberry bushes in your gardens and as alternatives to ornamental bushes. Nothing beats the sweetness and taste of a handful of plump blueberries in the morning as you walk your homestead. I have over thirty blueberry bushes spread out over my property, and I intend to increase those numbers. A great way to reduce harvest lost to animals is to have more fruit plants then you think you need.

There are two main things to keep in mind when you're growing blueberry bushes. The first is that they like soil that's more acidic. The second is to plant at least two different varieties. The plants will cross-pollinate each other, which leads to plumper blueberries and higher yields.

Plant blueberry bushes in full sun and in a place where water doesn't sit. They like well-draining soil. Blueberries prefer soil that is under a 6.0 pH; a soil test is the only way to accurately know what your soil pH level is in a planting area. Blueberry plants don't need to be overfertilized. So if your plants look yellow and aren't growing well, that's a sign that your pH level is probably too high. You'll need to reduce it by adding elemental sulfur or an acid-specific granular fertilizer.

An effective way to set up your planting hole for blueberry bushes is to use peat moss. Peat moss is acidic, and it will reduce the pH value of the soil. You can put four to five shovelfuls of peat moss into the planting area, mixing it well into the soil. That will help provide more acidity, lowering the soil's pH level in the immediate growing area. This will help your newly planted blueberry bush establish. You can also purchase water-soluble fertilizers for acid-loving plants. Water in your new transplants with this type of fertilizer and again every four to six weeks for the first season.

CANE FRUITS: RASPBERRIES AND BLACKBERRIES

Raspberries and blackberries are classic additions to homesteads. Where there were once a handful of wild varieties, there are now hundreds of new selections. Some gardeners like to grow original heritage canes and others love trying out the new varieties. Whatever you choose, they are a must-grow fruit crop. Blackberries and raspberries

should be planted in full sun and don't like to sit in standing water. As long as the soil drains well, they'll thrive. They are typically planted as single canes and need a full year before starting fruit production. They don't need much in the way of fertilizer, and they reproduce quickly. Most varieties of raspberries and blackberries tend to creep to spread across a space, sending up new canes, they can become invasive. I grow erect varieties of thornless blackberries, which send up new canes close to the original parent plant. I grow these blackberries inside my main garden as they tend to stay clumped and contained. They make great container plants too. I recommend planting them in 20-gallon (76 L) containers. They'll do well in that size container for many years. Raspberries, because of their spreading habit, are best planted along the edge of a wooded area that gets sun or in space where they can freely expand and create a large hedge.

Grapes

Grapes are very versatile. I am growing a Concord grape in a whisky half-barrel container. It's growing out of the barrel along my fence line. They are cold-hardy and can be pruned and maintained in small space. Grapes can be prone to diseases, but those can be managed well with organic copper sprays. Setting up a spraying schedule will help keep grapes healthy and thriving. I have several different grape varieties growing in different parts of my garden. I recommend starting with a seedless variety; 'Thompson' is a delicious seedless variety used in making raisins. 'Lakemont' is a smaller white seedless grape that's very sweet. There are many varieties to choose from, and it's worth looking them over. Many varieties have disease resistance, too, if your area carries problems for grapes.

Fruit and Nut Trees

Fruit and nut trees come in dwarf varieties and can be planted in containers. You can grow full-sized varieties if you have the space but consider how large they get and how you'll need to prune and manage them. Some fruits, such as apples, plums, and pears, need other varieties to cross-pollinate them. Others are self-pollinating. Some fruit and nut trees have great disease resistance, but others are quite susceptible to disease. I am growing fourteen fruit trees across my homestead. The 'Fiji' apple tree is handling disease the best out of all four apple trees. The 'Contender' peach tree yields the sweetest peaches I've ever tasted. My fruit trees are planted as a mini orchard along my fence line, and I even have dwarf varieties inside my main garden. I recommend buying trees in containers and not bare root. The bare-root trees are less expensive, but the extra money spent purchasing fruit or nut trees that are 4 to 5 feet (1.2 to 1.5 m) tall with a rootball is worth it.

Rely on Local Growers

It's well worth your time to visit local nurseries and ask them what varieties of fruit and nut trees, as well as other fruiting plants, do best in your area. When we talked about disease prevention and problem solving, you learned that finding out what grows well in your area saves you time, headaches, and heartaches. Local community nurseries have the knowledge to help you select the right fruit or nut tree for your homestead. Choosing the right variety is golden. Fruit and nut trees can take two to three years to produce. If they're plagued by diseases and problems, that's quite a lot of time lost if you need to replace them.

Now that you know how to set up your homestead garden and grow a plethora of edible plants, let's take a look at how to harvest, preserve, and prepare a few of these homegrown foods.

10

USING THE HOMESTEAD HARVEST

THERE'S NOTHING I ENJOY MORE THAN picking homegrown crops from the garden. Freshly picked is always better because you're harvesting vegetables that are full of moisture and sugars. Once picked, they begin to dehydrate, the sugars are converted to starches, and the flavors change. That's why vegetables from a grocery taste differently than fresh-picked produce. Once my garden starts producing, I walk through it several times a day and pick what's fresh. My harvest becomes the ingredients for my breakfast, lunch, and dinner. My first stop is my garden and edible landscape; the second is the grocery store. Over time, you'll begin to make fewer stops at grocery stores.

What you can't eat fresh will have to be stored or preserved for future use, and it certainly is wonderful to eat homegrown during winter, when our gardens are "closed." In this chapter, we'll cover my favorite techniques for easily preserving your harvests

Cool Storage

Winter squash, onions, garlic, cabbages, and other vegetables store well in cool temperatures. Roots cellars were mainstays of most homes before refrigeration. Cool storage is something to consider as space becomes available. Some vegetables are even stored with their roots on. You can clean and rinse the roots of kale and collard plants and store them on slatted shelves or in metal ring baskets that allow air circulation. Once stored, your vegetables begin to lose water, but storage areas with higher humidity help slow this process. Root cellars are kept dark to stop photosynthesis of leafy plants. The general temperature range for cool storage is 40°F to 55°F (4°C to 13°C). Vegetables such as onions, potatoes, and garlic can store well at warmer temperatures, too, and can even sit in baskets at room temperature.

VEGETABLES THAT STORE WELL

Onion (Let cure 5–7 days outside)
Garlic (Let cure 5–7 days outside)
Potato (Let cure 5–7 days outside)
Carrot
Turnip
Beets
Cabbage
Pumpkin (Let cure 7 days outside)
Winter Squash (Let cure 7 days outside)
Beans (Left to dry on the vine and stored)
Curing is letting outdoors temperature dry them, once harvested or picked.

Canning, Pickling, and Freezing

Other ways to store vegetables include canning, which is an elaborate process beyond the scope of this book. Pressure canning systems are available and they allow your homestead harvest to be stored in glass jars, no refrigeration needed. This is a skill worth mastering, and one I'm currently working on. Pickling is the process of storing vegetables jarred in an acidic brine. Brines are typically made with white vinegar, which is 5 percent acetic acid. This is a common dilution level for many manufactured vinegars. Brines are best made with 50 percent vinegar and 50 percent water. You can use 100 percent vinegar if your taste allows, but always pickle with at least 50 percent vinegar. Its acidity prevents harmful bacteria from growing. I also recommend refrigerating your pickled products. (I have a separate refrigerator for this.)

BASIC PICKLING

You can pickle cucumbers for classic pickles, but you can also pickle just about anything else. Chop any vegetables or combinations you want to pickle into bite-sized pieces. Minced garlic and onions are mainstays for flavor, but they can be omitted based on taste preferences. Herbs, salt, pepper, and other seasonings can be mixed in

endless combinations. I make my pickling seasoning in a bowl and add it to the jars, one at a time.

Boil the chopped vegetables slightly to soften them and prepare them for the brine. This process is called "blanching." Bring a pot of water to a boil, drop in the cut vegetables for 1 to 2 minutes, and remove. Put them in ice water immediately to stop the cooking process. Fill the bottom of an empty jar with some minced garlic and onions to taste and add the amount of pickling season you want per jar. (All jars and lids should be sterilized in boiling water before filling them.) Fill the jar with the vegetables, leaving about ½ inch (1 cm) of space at the top. Once the vegetables are jarred, add a 50/50 mixture of white vinegar and water and seal the jars. You can make hot brines and use that to fill your jar, but I prefer this method. For best storage use the 50/50 ratio and refrigerate immediately. Since they're not canned in a hot water bath or a pressure canner, they must be refrigerated at all times.

FREEZING

Freezing in sealed bags is a great way to store sauces. I use this as my main method for processing tomatoes and enjoying them in fall and winter. I recommend a double sealed freezer bag for sauces. Chopped kale and collards freeze nicely and are great out of the freezer for smoothies, soups, and mixed with potatoes or rice. I will chunk up squash, zucchini, eggplant, and onions, and freeze them for making future soup stocks and sauces. When I make sauces, I often add squash, pumpkins, onions, and even eggplants. You don't have to stick to the standard tomato sauce. Pastas are delicious dressed with all kinds of vegetable-based sauces and sautéed vegetables.

My Method for Making Vegetable Sauces

Tomatoes are my favorite vegetable to grow. I can easily grow hundreds of pounds of tomatoes, which certainly outpaces my ability to eat or give them away. I like making a rustic tomato sauce and freezing it flat in zip-top bags. This is a great way to quickly preserve and store your produce. You can add other vegetables into the sauces such as

Simple Sautés and Pasta Primavera

There are so many different ways to cook your homestead harvests. Like gardening, I cook from guidelines, but I don't really follow recipes. Let's start with a basic sauté. It isn't fancy, but it's very versatile and can be used with most crops. This is a sauté I make when peas are ready for harvesting. You'll find ingredients change as your garden does, keeping dinner fresh and full of new flavors.

Start by thinly slicing the onion and then cutting it into ½-inch (1 cm) pieces. Heat a frying pan on medium and add 2 to 3 tablespoons (15 to 30 ml) olive oil. Drop in the onions (but hold the salt and seasonings until the end). Sauté for 10 to 15 minutes until they're translucent. If you want, add a finely minced clove of garlic when the onions are nearly done. This is the base for most of the sautés I make. I even make notes when I cook and refer back to them when I try new things.

Add some red peppers, sliced long and thin, and your pea pods. What I sauté varies on what I am harvesting. I like growing snow peas and snap peas as both pods are edible. Sauté for another 5 to 10 minutes and add salt, pepper, and 1 to 2 tablespoons (15 to 30 ml) of butter toward the end. The longer you sauté, the softer the vegetables get, so check them for texture and taste. This is delicious when mixed with pasta or as a simple side dish. If you're mixing it with pasta, dress the pasta with olive oil and additional butter if you don't mind the calories. Just mix all together and you'll have simple version of a pasta primavera. You can add cheese to top it off and more garden herbs. I also mix sautéed vegetables with rice. I highly recommend mastering a sauté. You'll use it weekly when the homestead garden is producing like crazy!

eggplant, squash, zucchini, onions, and peppers. You can make different sauces with different flavors and store them all winter. My sauces are made from whatever is harvest-ready out of the gardens.

I love tending to my garden and growing vegetables, but I don't overly enjoy canning or processing all the produce. I just don't always have the time. Over the years, I came up with a way to quickly make tomato sauce without having to peel, de-seed, and can. This process is really easy. All you need is an immersion blender that can go into hot liquids.

EASY 4-STEP TOMATO SAUCE

Step 1: Cut up tomatoes (however many you have on hand) and drop them into a large pot. You can add other vegetables at your pleasure. Don't season your sauce at this point.

Step 2: Bring the tomatoes to a slow, rolling boil (without a lid); then turn the heat to simmer to reduce your sauce to about one-third of its starting volume. Let it thicken through evaporation until it looks like pasta sauce. If you had seasoned it with salt and pepper when it was full of liquid, it would be overly salty. The right amount of salt when a sauce is full of liquid is way too much once it reduces. Save seasoning for the end, once the reduction is complete.

Step 3: Once your sauce has reduced, use an immersion blender to thoroughly process your tomatoes and other vegetables into a fine purée.

Step 4: Let it simmer and reduce for several more hours to thickness of your liking. Season as desired at this point. The result will be an amazing and delicious pasta sauce.

Air Drying Herbs

Your freshly picked herbs can be dried and stored to be used over the season. The key to drying herbs is slow and low as to keep the essential oils and flavor in the dried leaves. Cut bunches of basil, oregano, thyme, chives, and other herbs, early in the morning after the dew has dried, to hang and dry. The general rule of thumb is to leave one-third of the plant for regrowth. Tie one end of each bunch with cotton or jute twine and hang to dry. Tie them tightly or use a rubber band around the ends as the stems will shrink as they dry. This can be done outdoors, under a fully shaded structure, that will protect the herb bunches from rain. They can also be hung indoors away from direct sunlight. Drying time will vary, taking several days to weeks. You want the leaves to be completely dried before storing them.

Herbs should be stored in airtight bags or containers. They can be stored with the leaves on the stem or you can remove the leaves and roughly crush them up as you wish. I like to use different sized Mason jars to store my herbs. The general conversion for use is 1 teaspoon (5 ml) of dried herbs to 1 tablespoon (15 ml) of fresh herbs. Dried herbs keep their flavor for about one year.

Good Luck on Your Homestead Gardening Journey!

I am so excited for you and hope you start your homestead garden journey soon. Start small, learn, and build toward your dreams. You'll become more skilled every year. One day, you'll look back and truly appreciate your decision to become more self-sufficient and self-reliant. That small orchard will be huge and your gardens will have expanded. You will always have a place to pause, reflect, and understand what life is all about as you walk your homestead. Your garden will give back to you; all you have to do is help it along. Cheers!

Acknowledgments

To my Grand-Pop: You taught me how to plant my first garden and helped me discover my never-ending passion for growing vegetables. You are forever present.

To my parents: You gave me love and a life that allowed me to follow my passion.

To my wife, Angela: Thanks for always being there and allowing me to dream, build, and track dirt everywhere.

About the Author

Gary Pilarchik grew up in southern New Jersey, the Garden State. He found a passion for gardening at an early age and rediscovered it in Maryland while raising his children, Jenna and Alec, with his wife, Angela. He is a retired mental health therapist and creator of The Rusted Garden Homestead. He and his wife are currently living in an 1867 farmhouse on 2 acres, where he is actively building his gardens and edible landscape.

His passion led him to making his first garden YouTube video in 2011. He now has over 1,000 videos, created to teach and help people enjoy their gardens and lives.

If you want to reach Gary, he can be found at:

Garden & Seed Shop: therustedgarden.com
Email: therustegarden@gmail.com
The Rusted Vegetable Garden Blog: therustedgarden@blogspot.com

And he can be found on YouTube, Instagram, TikTok, and other social media under The Rusted Garden.

Index

Also Available

The Complete Guide to No-Dig Gardening
978-0-7603-6791-9

No-Waste Composting
978-0-7603-6870-1

Complete Container Herb Gardening
978-0-7603-6779-7

The Plant Propagator's Bible
978-0-7603-6979-1